# Religion Industrial Complex

# in

# Indonesia

No part of this book may be used or reproduced in any form whatsoever without written permission from the author.

This book is a work of non fiction.

*Religion Industrial Complex in Indonesia*

ISBN 978-1-304-89063-4

To my beloved family;

Father, mother, and younger siblings

This is just a beginning.

*"Capital is money, capital is commodities. By virtue of it being value, it has acquired the occult ability to add value to itself. It brings forth living offspring, or, at the least, lays golden eggs"*

*– Karl Marx*

Our world breed an economically consumptive market where greedy capital players continuously target a vast amount of productive middle class to be leeched out of their hard earned money and spend it on whatever goods their mega-companies are producing. Most of these CEOs apparently would not miss the opportunity to exploit social trends, even ideological or cultural related behavior and beliefs of their prospective consumers – and they are not afraid broadening their scope to touch sensitive issues like, for example, religion. The expansion does not end here, however, as they further studying these issues in order to learn important variables, to be exploited later for their beneficiary use. What makes subject like religion gain a spotlight in the eyes of these capital players? One thing for sure is that money knows no boundaries. Even nonmaterial things such as ideas, norms, values, and even beliefs can be tagged with a price.

Karl Marx wrote that capital *has acquired the occult ability to add value to itself*. The words *"occult"* here could emphasize that everything, even the most unrealistic thing, will always have a value. Through money – which has its own value too – the bridge of possibility in selling commodities to all existing sectors in this world is crossable. Various sectors are already exploited and some are yet to be discovered, and religion apparently qualified as one of those *"golden eggs"* Marx described. However, one would not recklessly jump into this sector without first understand how much this sector could affect the mass and how much profit they will gain by utilizing it. Now let's quote another words from Marx concerning religion:

*"Religion is the sigh of the oppressed creature, the heart of a heartless world, just as it is the spirit of a spiritless situation. It is the opium of the people." – Karl Marx5*

Further more in Marx (1843) [1] contribution in *Critique of Hegel's Philosophy of Right,* he added that religion as the *illusory* form happiness can be easily constructed in people's mind because they are longing for the real happiness government cannot provide. Therefore, eradicating this belief appears to be quite difficult as globalization and modernization itself could not stand a chance against the statistically increasing religious believers and altering people mind from the illusory happiness of religion would be pointless if the real happiness they desire cannot be achieved or provided.

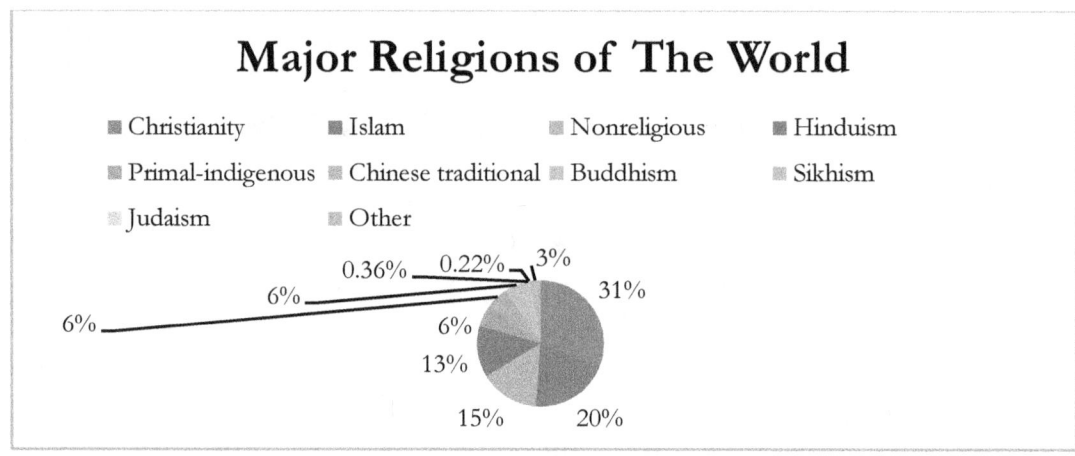

**Source:** *http://www.adherents.com (2005)*

From the chart above, we can clearly see that the *nonreligious* sector only count for 15 percents of all the population in the world (according to adherents.com data). This fact alone is enough to justify the idea of which religion can be used for beneficial purpose; from the simple act like marketing specific products, to the extreme extent such as controlling the people. In the economic side, knowing that religious population dominating the world could possibly exploited to increase their company sales. Laurence R. Iannaccone (1998) in *Introduction to the Economics of Religion* wrote that studies of religion can enhance the possibility of economic increase by reaching to the neglected area of *nonmarket* behavior, which means by studying their religious behavior, company can adapt and modified their products or service to match these type of consumers. But this beneficiary obtained from religion does not limit to the consumer goods. Religion, as previously stated by Marx can also be exploited for political purpose to those who seek power and control over the people. His theory of religion from *On Religion* (Marx and Engels, 1975)[2] explained that even though religion is not the product of capitalism, as it already existed before capitalism, the religious followers are not aware that the capitalists take serious interest to gain profit from it, thus makes religion very vulnerable of being commoditized.

---

[1] http://www.marxists.org/archive/marx/works/1843/critique-hpr/intro.htm

[2] http://hirr.hartsem.edu/ency/Marx.htm

Indonesia, being one amongst the other third world developing countries in Southeast Asia, has also acknowledged for its statistically massive religious believers. From 2005 census data conducted by *Biro Pusat Statistik* (BPS), it was discovered that the major religion followed by Indonesians is Islam as showed on the chart below:

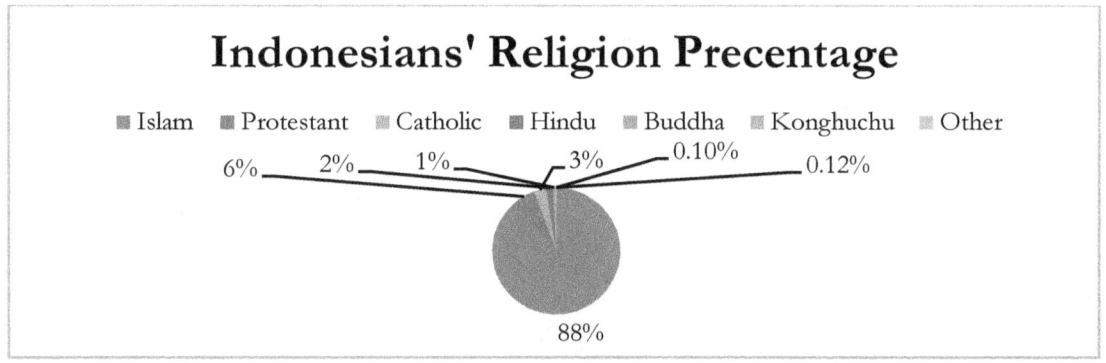

**Source:** Center for Religious and Cross-cultural Studies (CRCS). *Laporan Tahunan Kehidupan Beragama Di Indonesia Tahun 2008*. Universitas Gadjah Mada

It is evident that the big number of 88% are representing the majority of Indonesia's citizen, therefore those who has access to this large population would surely benefit for whatever their main purpose is. This very situation reminds us of the old quotes by a famous author;

> *The control of information is something the elite always does, particularly in a despotic form of government. Information, knowledge, is power. If you can control information, you can control people.* — *Tom Clancy*

Now let's replace the words *"information"* with *"religion"*; wouldn't it sound more promising? Concerning that the *other* sector (which is included for *non* believers) only count for 0.10% thus in order to conquer this country, all they have to do is control the 88%. The ruling class would not stop exploiting the sub-dominant, utilizing even the least apparent crack, to profit and maintain their hegemony.

## What Makes this Issue Problematic

What makes this issue stand out is that besides the usage of religion in economic sector, ignoring the fact that religion is vulnerable and have rather *surreal* traits such as non materialized and mostly comes from *tell-tales* without legitimate proof yet; the people with capital interest still taking advantage in utilizing it, while the followers of the religion are not aware that they are being manipulated. More views on how this non-substantive dysfunction of religion, Marx (Marx and Engels, 1976) in *The German and Ideology* described that religion could attach legitimacy to ideas, making them publicly viewed as sacred thus granting the ruling class a serious economic position and maintain their hegemony.

The exploitation of religion's non-substantive dysfunction by the ruling class through hegemony, which was explained by Gramsci in Haugaard and Lentner (2006) book called *Hegemony and Power: Consensus and Coercion in Contemporary Politics*, described that the elites in legal or *subliminal* way are exploiting sub-dominant class for profitable purpose. Gramsci believed that bourgeois domination could be effectively achieved without coercive acts such as military or economic force, but instead with regularly planned consensus within all the sub-dominant class. This social hegemony operates through society's superstructure, planting ideas to institution, conscious penetration, and cultural process in order to make people accept the ideal vision which the elites proposed.

This hegemonic exploitation to society, even though without coercive persuasion is resulting numerous victims. Disinformation through forcing schematic consciousness planted by the elites is sacrificing the oblivious people; religious organizations with hidden agenda are built, masking their true intentions of benefitting the ruling class. These kinds of organizations are rapidly growing in every part of the world, mostly in third world countries where religious followers statistically higher than advanced ones.

Besides creating *malicious* religious organizations to gain mass, ruling class also taking advantage of the military industry in order to profit themselves financially. For example in *war on terror* case, with intense growth on radical Islamist group and the continuously planted ideas that *"terrorism is wrong thus we have to do all we might to eliminate it"*, government have legitimate reason to purchase military and defense related technology and recruiting unnecessary number of human resources. Quoting from Quinney (1979) in *Criminal Justice – Industrial Complex* theory, the symbiotic relationship between government and industry will always running in motion with the rapidly growing monopoly.

If we study Marx's class pyramid, this *unholy* mutualism between ruling class and their tools cannot be separated as they are supporting each other for the whole system to succeed. In the chart below, Marx clearly pointed that the elites situated at the top, along with *Relations of Productions* which also included religion and *Forces of Productions* or what we usually call sub-dominant or oblivious wage slaves:

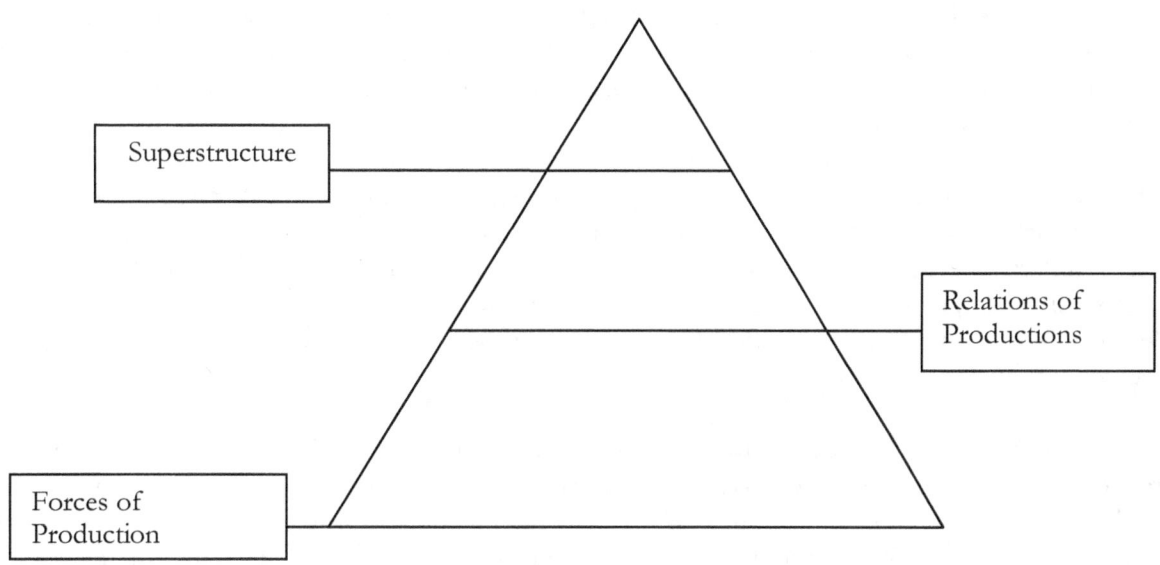

**Source:** *http://business.baylor.edu/Steve_Gardner/KarlMarx1.html*

This class structure pyramid applies to every single part of the world, but the most apparent hierarchy gap comes from Southeast Asia countries, mostly the developing and third world ones, in this case: Indonesia.

Elites has been maintaining their hegemony and cultivating capital profit at the same time by constructing and executing *malicious* scheme using religion as a tool, to control the people. Here in this so-called democratic country we could find religious organizations clashing against each other, even when they come from the same religious background. Religious political parties are built to gain followers for political purpose and we can also find a ministry working specially for religion business: Ministry of Religion. The fact that religious business is very promising here, elites can harvest huge amount of capital profit; exploiting and forcing their idea to masses with religion as a tool, while the people are unaware of this hegemonic violence.


> *"The challenge of modernity is to live without illusions*
> *and without becoming disillusioned".*
>
> *– Antonio Gramsci*


Several cases and examples of how religion dysfunction utilized for whatever goals the elites might desired to achieve can be found on various research, including the one conducted by D. Michael Lindsay (2008) titled *Evangelical in the Power Elite: Elite Cohesion Advancing a Movement*. The research by Lindsay examines American evangelical social movements as proletariat phenomenon with public leaders and elite actors also joined in playing the significant roles. Through prearranged interviews gathered from 360 elite informants (governments/politics, arts/entertainment/media, religion, nonprofit/social sector, higher education, business/corporate life), as well as archival and ethnographic research, Lindsay found the mechanisms of how the leaders advanced their evangelicalism between 1976 and 2006. These public leaders formed organizations, networks, power, and positioned themselves in both formal and informal authority to achieve their movement goals. After finding out the result, it appeared that significant religious identity and cohesive networks have played important roles in determining the goals and ambitions of leaders within the evangelical organizations. Religious identity played a vital role inside the structure of elite power, and evangelicals could bring social change.

From this very research, Lindsay also mentioned Marx's *The German Ideology* where he argued that capitalist class controls not just the economic area, but also the political and ideological areas to such degree that *"the ideas of the ruling class are in every epoch the ruling ideas."* Economic powers gather a ruling group of capitalists, granting their domination towards the masses. Besides Marx's view about the ruling class and their power to rule the masses, Lindsay added Mosca's argument from *The Ruling Class* which implied about his agreement of Marx's view and that there are two type of classes: those who rule and those who are ruled, but he argued that in this matter, social power does not lay in the hand of capitalists but instead it belongs to society's political leadership. There are another alternative model of elite power, however, that argues about how modern society is highly differentiated, thus it cannot produce unified harmony among those who inhabit authoritative positions. This view was originally come from Weber but explicated by Dahl (1958) and Keller (1963). They stated that power is circulated geographically, among assorted sectors, and across several entities. Keller also differentiates the strategic elites and a ruling class in terms of recruitment, internal organization, and degree of specialization.

Another confirmation on how religion and politics in fact affecting each other come from Dwight B. Bilings and Shauna L. Scott (1994) research from *Religion and Political Legitimation*. They examined the double function of religion in both the legitimation of power and privilege, and also in protest and opposition even though theories of secularization and modernization predicted the declining significance of religion in contemporary public life such as one argued by Parsons (1964) which posited lingering but indirect role for religious legitimation through institutional differentiation and value generalization but Berger (1967) described seemingly inexorable processes of secularization and privatization, and Bellah (1970) asserted that *"standards doctrinal orthodoxy and attempts to enforce moral purity [had] largely been dropped"* from modern religious life.

In this research Bilings and Scott reviewed new approaches to religious activism and legitimation efforts in the United States and in the world-system that stress the interrelatedness of religion and politics. Religion dual purpose as *"apology and legitimation of the status quo and its traditions of inequality on the one hand, and as a way of disapproval, revolutionize, and liberty on the other hand"* was mentioned by Solle (1984). In another synbook, Marx, Weber, and Durkheim, Berger (1967) described religion as both *"world-maintaining"* and *"world-shaking"* strength competent of legitimating or challenging supremacy and privilege. Billings and Scott research shows that religious activism and its role in political legitimation indeed affecting the struggles over power and privilege, both in the United States and elsewhere.

Besides political use in exploiting the religious dysfunction, it appears that religion can also be utilized in causing conflict and it is due to the significant role modernization posed towards the society. Jonathan Fox (2004) in *Religion and State Failure: An Examination of the Extent and Magnitude of Religious Conflict from 1950 to 1996* explained that few cross-sectional studies have examined the degree to which in-house conflict since World War II has been religious, and those that have done so are restricted in either the type of conflict or time span they cover. In this research, Fox use the State Failure data set to review whether the relative and absolute number of religious conflicts since World War II has increased, whether these conflicts are more severe than other conflicts, and whether any particular religions contribute in conflict more often than others. Religious conflicts often tend to be more intractable due to the non-bargainable nature of the motivations behind them. Wentz (1987) calls this phenomenon *"walls of religion."* People build walls around their belief systems and defend them at all cost.

The discovery of Fox's research show that while taking place less often than other types of conflicts, religious conflicts have amplified between 1950 and 1996, and are more powerful than nonreligious conflicts. Fox mentioned Lambert (1999) who argues that modern factors, including reason, science, individualism, mass participation in politics, capitalism, and globalization, have changed both the nature of religion and its role in society. Religious knowledge is more reachable to individuals and to be found in the framework of knowledge from other sources. As a result, religion has become both less significant and has moved from the public to the private area. This has made the partition of church and state as well as increase in individual freedom of choice over religious issues amplified. Beyer (1999) counters Lambert's argument and stated that the role of religion in society and politics might very well changed due to modernity, but its influence has not disappeared. Swatos and Christiano (1999) also added that religiosity has not declined and religion still has an influence.

Religion is experiencing a resurgence or revitalization due to a number of factors inherent in modernity:

1. In many parts of Third World, efforts at modernization have failed causing a religious backlash against the western secular ideologies which were the basis for the

governments which were in charge of these unsuccessful efforts at modernization (Juergensmeyer, 1993; Thomas, 2000).

2. Modernization has undermined traditional lifestyles, community values, and morals, which are based in part on religion, thus contributing to this religious backlash against modernity (Sahliyeh, 1990; Haynes, 1994; Thomas, 2000).

3. Modernization has allowed both state and religious institutions to increase their sphere of influence, thus resulting in more clashes between the two (Shupe, 1990).

4. Modern political system allow for mass participation in politics, which has allowed the religious sectors of society a means to impose their views on others (Rubin, 1994).

5. Modern communications have allowed religious groups to export their views more easily and the international media has made religious groups aware of the activities of other religious groups, often inspiring similar actions (Shupe, 1990).

6. Rational choice or economic theory of religion argues that the freedom of choice in many modern societies to select one's own religion has led to an increase in religiosity (Iannaccone, 1995).

7. In many parts of the Third World, due to the process of colonialism and cultural colonialism, western secular ideas are considered foreign and, therefore, illegitimate, leaving only religion as a basis for legitimacy (Juergensmeyer, 1993).

8. Modern religious organization contributes to political activity. On general level, some form of organization is necessary for political mobilization. Religious institutions provide ready-made organizations for this purpose, which often have access to the media, considerable economic assets, and international communication network (Fox, 1999; Hadden, 1987; Harris, 1994; Johnston and Figra, 1988; Verba et al., 1993).

In terms of hegemonic aspect of religion, Dwight B. Bilings (1990) in *Religion as Opposition: A Gramscian Analysis* writes analytical research builds on Antonio Gramsci's approach to the dynamics of hegemony and counterhegemony, develops guidelines for the historical analysis of the conditions under which religion promotes either social quiescene or opposition. Bilings stressed Gramsci's argument about the importance of leadership resources and organizational autonomy for oppositional movements, as well as social-psychological studies of the processes of religious conversion and commitment bring to light the importance of social support for the plausibility of belief. Using the three factors above, Bilings examined oppositional movements of coal miners and textile workers in the American South after World War I and proves that religion is a crucial factor in either blunting or heightening worker's insurgency.

Using Durkheim (1965), Parsons (1964), and Wilson (1982) to stress the positive contribution of religion to maintain the social order, Bilings points out that religion still has to be understood regarding its *"double function"* capability. He then described how religion has direct effect on activism. Religion neither *"sparked the slaves to rebellion nor rendered them docile"* (Gevovese, 1976) but rather religion functions as a relatively autonomous sphere of social life that acts as a mediating variable between oppression and opposition or submission. Billings also mentioned Gramsci's model of class-based opposition to interpret historically which side religious leaders were in industrial conflicts and concluded that:

1. Religion is not a *"superstructural"* reflection of material interests but rather as a mediating variable in social conflicts, it has both a degree of autonomy and material impact.

2. Whether religious leaders defend the hegemony of dominant social groups or contribute to the creation of an oppositional culture depends on the development of what Gramsci called critical understanding which dependent on three mutually supportive conditions:

   a. Autonomous organizations that allow room for reflection independent of the ideological presuppositions of the dominant group.
   b. Organic intellectuals who help to develop alternative worldviews that challenge the status quo and who work to educate movement participants.
   c. Social interactions among participants that sustain new worldviews and insure their plausibility.

3. In the case of class-based oppositional movements, religion may figure as a significant dimension of the politics of class formation.

Connecting religion, hegemony and class, Eugen Schoenfeld (1992) on *Militant and Submissive Religions: Class, Religion and Ideology* provides a good example on how every social class has their own ideology: (1) The religions of the ascending classes are primarily inclusive militants emphasizing the values of collectivity, equality and justice. (2) The religions of the retrenching classes are exclusive militants which stress individualism, freedom, and Christian love. (3) Bourgeois religions are inclusive submissive and while they incorporate the values of the above two, they also add the values of charity and decorum. (4) The religions of the alienated classes are exclusive submissive and anti-class although they do manifest a castle-like system with an elitist self concept and total commitment to the group. If one utilizing this knowledge about classes and its religious association, they would know how to conduct their hegemonic plan and control the social system or socialize their visions, with the intention of profiting from it.

To see more involvements of religion in political sphere, a research by Richard L. Wood (1999) titled *Religious Culture and Political Action* found religious institutions as generators of religious culture, presents as theoretical model of how religious cultural elements are incorporated into social movements and so shapes their internal political cultures and impacting the public realm. Wood argues that the content of an organization's culture matters greatly for political action, but in subtle and complex way. For example, *"religious culture"* in general does not necessarily enable or inhibit democratic political organizing but rather certain forms of religious culture enable such participation, and other forms of religious or secular culture constrain it.

Before reviewing the case of religion and political use in Indonesia, better see the general trend of this matter in Asian countries first. For example, review of Peter van der Veer's (2002) work called *Religion in South Asia*, which examines the condition of India from the angle of post colonialism criticism. The transformation of the public sphere in South Asia shows the increasing importance of religious movements and of the political use of religious images in new communication technologies. Veer mentioned Washbrook (1988) view which stated *"colonialism was the logical outcome of South Asia's own history of capitalist development."* In this research, media and social movements play significant role in communicating religious beliefs and practices and socializes new generations in them, as well as transmitting political views and language. The violent conflicts between Hindus and Muslims, between high castes and dalits, between Shi'as and Sunnis, between Buddhists and Hindus are also not regional, but increasingly global.

Another South Asian country which have the same religion and political issue as India is Bangladesh. Through *The Ubiquity of Islam: Religion and Society in Bangladesh*, Ahmed Shafiqul Huque and Muhammad Yeahia Akhter (1987) explains the resurgence of Islam in Bangladesh and various agents and forces within Bangladesh society that continually reinforce the place of Islam. In Bangladesh, the slightest aspersion on Islam results in hostile public reaction, which is why neither the government nor the opposition political parties speak out against Islam. Government announcements are often sprinkled with references to the establishment of Islamic values, and policies are determined in such a way as not to disturb this sensitive issue. The rulers have displayed a tendency to strengthen their base of power by exploiting the people's attachment to Islam. Huque and Akhter argue that party leaders are interested in joining the Islamic bandwagon to benefit their party policies and propaganda. Political parties try to capitalize on the Islamic sentiment, and successive rulers of Bangladesh have expressed their attachment to Islam in order to secure the support of the Muslim electorate. The present government also went a step further in exempting mosques from paying their electric and water-supply bills.

For Indonesia case, R. William Liddle (1996) with *The Islamic Turn in Indonesia: A Political Explanation* argues about ICMI or *Ikatan Cendekiawan Muslim Se-Indonesia* as an instrument designed and used by Presiden Suharto for his own purposes. In broad terms, it is a state corporatist organization (Schmitter, 1974) like many others created by the government during the New Order for the purpose of controlling important social groups. More specifically, it is a key element in a presidential drive to reassert direct control over the armed forces and to assure a massive victory for Golkar in the 1997 election and Suharto's own reflection as president in 1998. Moreover, Liddle explains that ICMI is an organization with Islamic name but with minimal Islamic content. It is led by state officials, handpicked at the top by Suharto himself, who do not subscribe to a militantly Islamic political ideology. Most of the members of the organization are also officials, and its funding comes directly and indirectly from the state. It does not have a specific, let alone an Islamic, policy or legislative agenda that its leaders are pledged to implement.

In the end, religion is a proven powerful political instrument. As explained by Raymond Firth (1981) in *Spiritual Aroma: Religion and Politics*, the strength of conviction of its followers, their certainty of the legitimacy of their premises, can lead to innovative action as well as political change instead of political support. The religion of a people, both in belief and in ritual, can symbolize their group identity irrespective of the particular structure of government and economy. A religious organization can provide a counterpoise to the authority of the state, a rallying point for people against unpopular decision or stressful conditions imposed by those in control. It is better to maintain the hegemony and prevent state chaos by controlling religion.

## Familiarize with "Religion Industrial Complex"

The term *Religion Industrial Complex* might not be familiar and perhaps (as far as research about this topic conducted) never before introduced as a whole distinct concept, thus in order to fully grasp the idea, let's first dive in to the concept which directly involves on how this Religion Industrial Complex terms arise; from the concept of society to how religion used by certain class.

***

## Society and Class Struggle

Chantal Mouffe (1979) on *Gramsci and Marxist Theory* explains the basic of civil society according to Karl Marx and Gramsci, which represents the active and positive moment of historical development. But still, in Marx, this active and positive moment is a structural moment, while Gramsci is superstructural. From the widely acknowledged work titled *"Manifesto of the Communist Party,"* Karl Marx with Frederick Engels (1848) described how society evolved from the feudal era to the modern industrial era with noticeable difference on each, but showed the exact form of bourgeoisie domination. In history we learned how class struggled against each other in open fight, with bare form of oppressions from the feudal lord to the lesser class of proletariat. Modern era, however, offers similar experience but slightly modified; with hidden schematic agenda, less oppression, and appears to be more peaceful.

*"Society as a whole is more and more splitting up into two great hostile camps, into two great classes directly facing each other – Bourgeoisie and Proletariat."*

*– Karl Marx*

The bourgeoisie played a very important part in industrial revolution; they offered a borderless relationship between men, put an end to feudal, patriarchal, idyllic relations. They introduced the concept of *"Free Trade"* where mass industrial production took place with cheap materials as their artillery thus making the value of a person is rated by its capital. However, even though there were no blatant display of slavery, bourgeoisie successfully created a mass form of wage labors to be exploited in such way it looked even more brutal than the slavery from feudal era. These wage labors, classified as proletariat, cannot be separated from the communist movement as the aim of their movement is to overthrow the bourgeoisie supremacy, making proletariat as the dominant class.

Hence, managing mass amount of wage labors while maintaining their submissive consciousness is not an easy job. Besides politics, there is also a tool powerful enough to legitimate the status quo: religion.

\*\*\*

## Religion

For Durkheim (1957) on his book *Professional Ethics and Civic Morals*, religion is a *'unified system of beliefs and practices relative to sacred things, that is to say, things set apart and forbidden – beliefs and practices which unite into one single moral community called a Church, all those who adhere to them.'* Wach (1944) listed the basic structural characteristics of religion such as: (1) Religious beliefs are to be interpreted as the 'collective representation' of society; (2) the unintended consequence of religious practices is to create a social bond; (3) the practice of religious rituals creates a social enthusiasm or 'effervescence' by which social commitments are renewed; (4) the training of the faithful in sacrifice and asceticism creates important norms of altruism and social service; (5) and religious mythologies, which are dramatically re-enacted in the ritual, store up the collective memory of the social group, without which the continuity of this historical narrative of generations would be impossible. In terms of function, according to Henry L. Tischer (2006) on *Introduction to Sociology*, religion has multiple of them, for example helping maintain the cohesion and social control, and furthermore to pleasure individuals' needs for emotional and spiritual comfort.

From *Religion's Place in Securing a Better World-Order,* James H. Tufts (1992) explained the three aspects of religion which are: (1) Ritual, very old tradition since the New Stone Age, traditions of the past to brings a sense of mystery and solemnity, also enhances and elevates emotion. The essence of ritual is to withdraw antagonisms and fierce passions, replace them with calm and peacefulness. (2) Old-Fashioned gospel, used to emphasize three things: a story of certain historic events of nineteen centuries ago; certain dogmas interpreting these events from metaphysical views; and the last one is certain emotional experiences undergone by the individual under these events and dogmas' influence. (3) Last aspect of religion is the power to change society, in a form of social revolution to contribute for the better world-order.

Religion maintains belief that there is moral freedom, moral responsibility, moral courage, and moral worth in a man and the universe is not merely an exclusive mechanism. Religion, further explained by Tufts, attempts to lift individual, races, and people from degradation and barbarism. But religion has another effect too. Karl Marx from the book *Marx on Religion* by John C. Raines (2002) stated that religion is opium of the people. Criticizing *Philosophy of Right* by Hegel, Marx argued that religion is an illusion which gives pleasure to the people in unfortunate social condition (poverty or unsatisfied at their condition) who needs happiness.

Now that we already pictured what religion is and what it is capable of, especially the ideas offered by Marx about its opium effect to the masses, the next possible logic to construct on why and how religion utilized is by examining its function on political area.

***

## Religion and Political Legitimation

From *Religion and Political Legitimation* by Dwight B. Billings and Shaunna L. Scott, religion described to have dual function: first was as apology and legitimation of the status quo and its culture of injustice, while the second was as a means of protest, change, and liberation (Solle, 1984). Berger (1967), synthesizing Marx, Weber, and Durkheim, also explained that religion as a force capable of legitimating or challenging power and privilege. This view is also supported by Bordieu (1987) from the *Spiritual Capital: Theorizing Religion with Bourdieu against Bourdieu* journal written by Bradford Verter (2003), which stated that religious power is capable of modifying the practice and world-view of lay people through the absolutization of the relative and legitimation of the arbitrary. He then added that the state use religion as ideological instrument for domination and they legitimizes it through social and political institutions.

Another view on how religion affects the political legitimation comes from a functionalist who described religious legitimation as *"control system[s] linking meaning and motivation"* (Bellah, 1970). Furthermore, Fenn (1974) also stated that religious legitimation as a *"process by which one aspect of a social system confers sanctions on society as a whole and on particular institutions within it."* Beckford (1983) offered more blatant view about this matter. He argued that religious legitimation as *"a sphere of activity where efforts are deliberately made to influence, manipulate, and control people's thoughts, feelings, and actions in accordance with various religious values."* Robert Wuthnow (1991) from *Understanding Religion and Politics* wrote about how government interfered and stepped in the religion business, devaluing the traditional religious institutions and offered rejuvenation to religion in order to tie societies together.

*"Gradually, this system became the driving force of modern capitalism, and its borders came to encompass most of the globe by the end of the nineteenth century."*

*— Robert Wuthnow*

Research conducted by D. Michael Lindsay (2008) published on the *Evangelicals in the Power Elite: Elite Cohesion Advancing a Movement* journal revealed that religious identity and cohesive networks apparently played vital roles in determining the goals and aspiration of leaders within the evangelical movement.

*"These public leaders founded organizations, formed networks, exercised convening power, and drew on formal and informal positions of authority to achieve movement goals." — D. Michael Lindsay*

The malice use of religion to settle the throne of power has been done through various means. Now how the bourgeoisie can inhabit their authority for extraordinarily long time? Elite settlements are quite important in order to achieve political stability, as stated by Michael G. Burton and John Higley (1987) on *Elite Settlements* journal. One of the most effective yet efficient for this elite settlement chore is by the course of *hegemony*.

\*\*\*

## Hegemony

Hegemony according to Gramsci from book written by Mark Haugaard and Howard H. Lentner (2006) called *Hegemony and Power: Consensus and Coercion in Contemporary Politics* described that the authority in legal or *subliminal* way, exploiting the lower class (sub-dominant) to achieve certain purpose which benefit them. Gramsci believed that bourgeois domination is possible to effectively achieved without any form of coercion like military or economic force, but instead with regularly planned consensus within all form of society. This social hegemony operates through society's superstructure, implant ideas to the people through institution, conscious penetration, and cultural process so people will accept the ideal visions the elite wanted.

There are three types of hegemony according to Perry Anderson (1977) based on Gramsci's *Prison Notebook* as listed in Robert Bocock's book of *Hegemony*:

1. First model, in terms of culture and morale leadership, hegemony was viewed to be placed in civil society; the state was coercive power's site in the form of police and military; and economy was a site for various work disciplines, related to cash, and monetary controls. The problem of this model was however, as explained by Anderson, hegemony was very much applied in the various states of western bourgeois nations as democratic parliamentary form. This condition made the sub-dominant class believed that they were really voted and decided their leader.

2. In the second model, hegemony was exercised at both state and civil society. Gramsci perceived that academic and law institutions were important in order to run the hegemonic scheme. This view on how the two most influential institutions have great role as hegemonic tools in civil society, is not necessarily false, as society takes these institutions importance very seriously. State gives their standards and ideas through academic and law institutions in order to maintain their hegemonic power over their citizen.

3. The third model of hegemony according to Gramsci was that there was no difference between state and civil society because Gramsci often addressed state as *Political Society* plus *Civil Society*. He added that state was not only referred to Government officials, but also *private sector* of *hegemony* or the civil society. Hegemony belonged to the private non-Government powers and also to the civil society which was also included in the *state* and thus a part of the *state*.

In *Producing Hegemony: State/Society Relations and the Politics of Productivity in the United States*, Mark Edward Rupert (1990) studied that liberal structure of state is a potential for maintaining hegemony. Rupert made example on how neoliberal constellation of public and private powers in the U.S was fundamental to accomplish the global power in both instrumental and substantive sense.

For the correlation between hegemony and religion, Ravindra K. Jain (1996) on *Hierarchy, Hegemony and Dominance: Politics of Ethnicity in Uttar Pradesh, 1995* quoted Weber:

> *"Any cultural trait, no matter how superficial can serve as a starting point for the familiar tendency to monopolistic closure..." – Weber*

Religion is also cultural trait, as it is passed down for many generations until this era. Therefore, in order to maintain the hegemony, one can utilize the power of religion and working towards political stability and whatever their aspirations might be.

## Structural Violence

Constructing the framework of *hegemony*, one would not miss the notion of its structural violence trait, conducted by the ruling class to sub-dominant. But before that, we have to understand the very basic definition of violence, as explained by Galtung (1969) on Peter Uvin (1998) book *Aiding Violence: The Development Enterprise in Rwanda*. Violence defined by galtung as *'those factors that cause people's actual physical and mental realizations to be below their potential realizations.'* However, on *Violence, Peace, and Peace Research* journal, Galtung (1969) also explains structural violence as a term firstly used on the 1960s era. That very term relates to a form of violence in a systemic technique where certain social structure or social institution harming people by preventing them to fulfill their needs. Institutionalization elite class, ethnocentrism, classism, racism, sexism, adultism, nationalism, heterosexism, and ageism are some example of structural violence. The effect of structural violence are often includes immediate violence, including family violence, racial violence, hate crime, terrorism, genocide, and war. From *Violence: Reflection on a National Epidemic*, James Gilligan (1997) defining structural violence as:

> *"The increased rates of death and disability suffered by those who occupy the bottom rungs of society, as contrasted with the relatively lower death rates experienced by those who are above them."*

\*\*\*

## Symbolic Violence

According to Bordieu, as written in *Constitutive Criminology: The Maturation of Critical Theory* (Stuart Henry, Dragan Millovanovic; *Criminology* Volume 29 Number 2; 1991), symbolic violence is a form of domination that is exerted through the very medium in which it is disguised, wherein it is the *"gentle, invisible form of violence, which is never recognized as such, and is not so much undergone as chosen, the violence of credit, confidence, obligation, personal loyalty, hospitality, gifts, gratitude, piety…"* but criminologists have forgotten this dimension of domination. The silence of the present and the celebration of that aspect that is likened to be law constitute the forms of control that appear as reality. Suppressed by silence, this pervasive domination is itself frozen in the past as *custom, pre-law,* and the *law* of multiplex relation.

## Criminal Justice Industrial Complex

Now that *society, political legitimation, religion* and *hegemony* already described, the relations between them needs to be found in order to explain this concept of *Religion Industrial Complex*. Basically, the idea of this concept comes from Richard Quinney's *Criminal Justice Industrial Complex*, which in the book titled *Criminology* he wrote about criminal justice industrial complex as a phenomenon where criminal justice is used for business opportunity with unnecessary purchases of criminal prevention tools and technology. Symbiotic relationship between government and industrial sector will always maintained in motion with the expanding monopoly sector. This argument was backed up by *Corrupt Exchanges: Actors, Resources, and Mechanism of Political Corruption: Social Problems and Social Issues* written by Donatella Della Porta and Alberto Vannucci (1999) which described about the phenomenon occurring in developing countries where there is indeed a relation between corruption and economic development. On *Punishment for Sale: Private Prisons, Big Business, and the Incarceration Binge*, Donna Selman and Paul Leighton (2010) define Criminal Justice Industrial Complex as prison industrial complex plus all those who supply goods or consulting to police departments and private security firms. Some of the firms were also part of the military industrial complex that transformed into criminal justice industrial complex. The similarity of criminal justice industrial complex and military industrial complex also approved by Byron Eugene Price (2006) from *Merchandizing Prisoners: Who Really Pays for Prison Privatization?* Regarding prison industrial complex, Schlosser (1998) identifies it as being substantially larger than private prisons. It includes all those who supply goods and consulting to jails, prisons, parole, and probation.

Perceiving Quinney's view about how criminal justice dysfunction exploited into some industrial *disease*, the term *Religion Industrial Complex* surfaced. Religion, which carried an important role as criminal justice, can also be utilized due to its *non-substantial* dysfunction. The dysfunction which is discoursing here is not the substantive element such as fundamental faith and belief system or its teachings, but instead the economical tendencies that can be potentially used based on the religion followers' statistic.

\*\*\*

## Introductory of Religion Industrial Complex

According to the previous statement that this concept is never before introduced, and as related to the aim of this book to discourse this phenomenon, then a rather moderate picture about this term is still needed in order to progress to the main research. Based on the fragments of Gramsci's *hegemonic* related ideas such as the three models of hegemony and the original concept adapted from Quinney's *Criminal Justice Industrial Complex*, it is clear that religion can be exploited economically by the state or private sector for capital gain. Thus, in order to make their business or we should say *industrial complex* run smoothly, civil society and mostly the followers must not revolt and accept the way that they are being *cultivated* by their primordial religious leader whom of course relate themselves with either government or private sector. What primordial religious leaders and both private and governmental officials needs to keep the citizen (or religious followers) unaware of the exploitation is through well schemed and tactically constructed *hegemony*.

Examples of this Religion Industrial Complex concept in Indonesia can be seen in local media, there were several cases happened recently about religious organization using violence to profit. Therefore, a fragment of conception about the terms *Religion Industrial Complex* is that where religion's non-substantive dysfunction is exploited for capital gain, in businesslike manner, thus becomes a disease; a *complex*.

Discoursing Religion Industrial Complex, this book offers a postmodern approach in Criminology. Postmodern criminology is one of many emerging critical perspectives of criminology. Critical theories share the view that *inequality in power is causally related to the problem of crime*. From *Theoretical Criminology*, George Bryan Vold, Thomas J. Bernard, Jeffrey B. Snipes (2002) explain about Marxist theory of postmodern criminology. Marxist theories generally locate power in the ownership of the means of production, while postmodern theories *locate it in the control over language systems*. However, both perspectives imply that the *crime problem can only be solved if power arrangements are changed*. Getting to the root of the problem of crime, according to these perspectives, *requires social change at the most fundamental level*. The most distinguished part of these theories amongst others is the focus on *'what ought to be'* rather than *'what is,'* on the *ideal* rather than *real*. Critical theories are difficult to recapitulate for two reasons:

1. Their complexity leads to profound disagreements among different theorists within the same area.
2. Theorists in these areas may frequently change their own positions as their thinking develops.

***

## Postmodernism

From *Theoretical Criminology,* (George Bryan Vold, Thomas J. Bernard, Jeffrey B. Snipes; 2002) Modernism, according to Anthony Borgman (1992) is associated with *naturalistic approach*, including the view that *science is an objective process directed toward predicting and controlling the world*.

Postmodernist theories attempt to move beyond modernism by arguing that *all thinking and all knowledge are mediated by language*, and that language itself *is never a neutral medium*; language always privileges some points of view and disparages others. To a certain extent, postmodernists even attack scientific thinking because they *attempt to deconstruct privileged points of view*. At the same time, postmodernists seek out the disparaged points of view in order to make them more explicit and legitimate. The objective is not merely to tear down one point of view and replace it with another, but rather to come to situation in which different grammars can be simultaneously held as legitimate, so that there is a sense of the diversity of points of view without assuming that one is superior and the others are not.

Postmodernists therefore examine *the relationship between human agency and language in creating meaning, identity, truth, justice, power, and knowledge*. This relationship is studied through 'discourse analysis,' a method of investigating how sense and meaning are constructed in which attention is paid to the values and assumptions implied in language. Discourse analysis considers *the social position of the person who is speaking or writing in order to understand the meaning of what is said or written*, not an analysis of the social roles that people occupy. Rather, it considers *how language is embedded in these roles and how that language shapes and forms the way people in these roles think and speak*, also known as 'discursive subject positions.' Postmodernist criminologists point out that, once people assume one of these 'discursive subject positions,' then *the words that they speak no longer fully express their realities, but to some extent express the realities of the larger institutions and organizations*. For example when organization leader seen together or meet up with politician in a public place or organization members, from other point of view this situation might not peculiar at all, however postmodernist criminologist will try to understand both party's social role; why two significant people meet up purposely in public, and considering a possibility that there must be something they are aiming.

\*\*\*

## Constitutive Criminology

Constitutive criminology is an integrated critical approach to the analysis of crime and its control. From *Constitutive Criminology: an Overview of an Emerging Postmodernist School* by Gregg Barak, Stuart Henry and Dragan Milovanovic, constitutive criminology is an affirmative postmodernism, recognizing the co-production of crime by human subjects, and by the social and organizational structures that humans develop and endlessly (re)build. The essence of the constitutive argument is that crime and its control cannot be separated from the totality of the discursively ordered, structural and cultural contexts in which it is produced. Constitutive criminology provides a genealogical investigation of crime, criminologists, and criminology in their relations with human subjects, law and social order; addressing crime's interwoven connection with the wider complexity of social relationships through a synoptic analysis whereby crime is related to the *symbolic,* the *imaginary*, and the *real*. It is an open-ended approach proposing that human subjects are responsible for actively creating their world with others, a world which simultaneously acts back, shaping the subjects' own identity. Through social interaction involving language and symbolic representations, people identify and evaluate differences, construct categories, organize their activities to reflects those categories, and share a belief in the reality of that which is constructed.

Human subject, in constitutive criminology is seen as *recovering* because it is always striving for a final and certain state of being, but never arrives. The recovering human subject always has the potential to escape the cages of its own and others' constructions, not least by investing energy in new ones. The human *subject-as-offender* is viewed as "excessive investor" in the power to dominate others; they put energy into creating and magnifying differences between themselves and others. This investment of energy disadvantages, disables, and destroys others' human potentialities. On the other hand, the human *subject-as-victim* is viewed as a special case of the "recovering subject," still with untapped human potentiality but with a damaged faith in humanity. Victims are more entrenched; more disabled, and suffer loss. Victims suffer the pain of being denied their own humanity, the power to make a difference. The victim of crime is thus rendered a non person, a non human, or less complete being (Henry and Millovanovich, 1996). Each of the "subjects" of these multiple interpretations of crime may simultaneously be viewed as "objects" for domination. As objects, human subjects represent co-produced reflections of the multiple signifiers that are connected in chaotic and continuous ways.

From constructive criminology's view, crime is a socially constructed and discursively constituted legal category. It is a violent categorization of the diversity of human conflicts and transgressions into a single category "crime." It melts differences reflecting the multitude of variously motivated harms into a single entity or series of legal abstractions, such as "violent crime" or "property crime." People in relations taken to be "crimes," are in relations of inequality. They are, as discursively constituted human subjects, being disrespected; reduced from what they are, prevented from being what they might be. Thus, we define crime as:

> *"The expression of some agency's energy to make a difference on others, and it is the exclusion of those others, who in the instant are rendered powerless to maintain or express their humanity."* — Henry and Milovanovic (1996)

This agency may be comprised and energized by people, social identities (men, women, etc), groups, parties, institutions, the state, or even constitutive interrelational-sets. This is the root of why capitalism is criminogenic, why ours is a violent society. the activities of those who construct occasions for the deliverance of power is crime. It is crime because it takes from people any present dignity and, further, represses their attempt to change.

***

This research carried out in Qualitative approach. According to Wilhelmina C. Savenye and Rhonda S. Robinson on *Qualitative Research Issues and Methods: an Introduction for Educational Technologists*, qualitative research is defined as research devoted to developing an understanding of human systems, be they small, such as a technology-using teacher and his or her students and classroom, or large, such as a cultural system. Qualitative research studies typically include ethnographies, case studies, and generally descriptive studies. They often are called *ethnographies,* but these are somewhat more specific. Taken from *Qualitative Research Methods: A Data Collector's Field Guide* by Family Health International:

> *"The strength of qualitative research is its ability to provide complex textual descriptions of how people experience a given research issue. It provides information about the "human" side of an issue — that is, the often contradictory behaviors, beliefs, opinions, emotions, and relationships of individuals. Qualitative methods are also effective in identifying intangible factors, such as social norms, socioeconomic status, gender roles, ethnicity, and religion, whose role in the research issue may not be readily apparent. When used along with quantitative methods, qualitative research can help us to interpret and better understand the complex reality of a given situation and the implications of quantitative data."*

This research categorized as Qualitative Descriptive. Margarete Sandelowski (2000) *on Focus on Research Methods: Whatever Happened to Qualitative Description?* Explains that researchers conducting qualitative descriptive studies seek descriptive validity, or an accurate accounting of events that most people (including researchers and participants) observing the same event would agree is accurate, and interpretive validity, or an accurate accounting of the meanings participants attributed to those events that those participants would agree is accurate (Maxwell, 1992). Researchers conducting qualitative descriptive studies stay closer to their data and to the surface of words and events than researchers conducting grounded theory, phenomenological, ethnographic, or narrative studies. In qualitative descriptive studies, language is a vehicle of communication, not itself an interpretive structure that must be read.

However, since the whole phenomenon would be analyzed through postmodern paradigm, then this research also use discourse analysis. From *Constitutive Criminology: The Maturation of Critical Theory* by Stuart Henry and Dragan Milovanovic on *Criminology* (Volume 29, Number 2; 1991) explained that discursive practices produce texts (narratives constructions), imaginary constructions, that anchor signifiers to particular signifieds, producing a particular image claiming to be the reality. These texts become the semiotic coordinates of action, which agent recursively use and, in so doing, provide a reconstruction of the original form.

Primary data are collected through various literature writings (books, journals) and media publications (paper and internet based). Data which are gathered then analyzed according to theories and critical framework or concept explained in the previous chapter. Researcher found, during the data collecting, that even though some religious group has much article written about them, only several online media covers the news related to their political behavior. However, for analytical purpose and general news coverage, data can be acquired relatively easy be it coming from local or foreign source.

In this research, researcher found several obstacles, as well as a lot of superiorities which eased the process of data gathering and analyzing:

a.  Superiorities

1.  In term of content, this book offers a fresh approach, as far as researcher knows, never before 'Religion Industrial Complex' introduced as a concept. There is also another *fresh* term researcher use such as 'Religious Opportunist Group.' Besides the content, from the data gathering, researcher never really stumbled into major difficulties; all publications and texts are relatively easy to acquire. Especially with theories and concepts, international journals and books are available through several online source or physical location such as library.

b.  Limitations

Despite the unproblematic in data gathering, obstacles are also apparent in this research. Not all data can be acquired easily, in some case, like political affiliation and connection between religious groups and politicians, finding the news media which published the story are hard to find. Especially the major noteworthy online media, however, since online news media are growing rapidly this year, there are several less popular news media available with the data researched needs. Using postmodern paradigm and discursive analysis are also difficult in which researcher must focus on interpreting crime symbolism in order to read the pattern and find the real meaning behind the subjects' behavior

## Ulama and Pesantren

The existence of moslem scholar or *Ulama* in local terms, as legal scholars engaged in the several fields of Islamic studies who have completed several years of training and study of Islamic disciplines, cannot be separated from the history process of Islam establishment in Indonesia. Jajat Burhanudin and Ahmad Baedowi (2003) from *Transformasi Otoritas Keagamaan* wrote that Ulama are amongst the most meritorious in introducing Islam to Indonesian. They are the one who converted a lot of early Indonesian monarch, from Hinduism and Buddha to the religion of Islam. Moreover, in some case, Ulama role in ancient Java era were not only for Islamization of the rulers, but also to become the rulers themselves. Legend of *Wali Sanga* is a good example of how Ulama can also be the head of some territories.

Starting from the 19<sup>th</sup> century, the communal awareness of Ulama increased highly and stronger due to the institutionalization in the form of academic institution called *Pesantren*. These academic institutions had been growing rapidly across Indonesia until now. Dr. Endang Turmudi (2003) in his book titled *Perselingkuhan Kiai dan Kekuasaan* quotes Dhofier (1982) description of pesantren where this certain institution use traditional education system called *Bandongan* and *Sorogan*. Bandongan is similar to attending class in college where a lot of *santri* (pesantren students) are listening to the more general knowledge shared by senior santri or Ulama, while in sorogan they specifically discussing about specific knowledge the santri wants to develop. Bandongan usually have more santri attending than sorogan. In social scope, pesantren plays central role in spreading Islam, become a formal socialization agent where beliefs, norms, and values of Islam transmitted through teachings.

Pesantren survivability from the early 19 century era until present time, even with the nonstop attack from modernization, globalization, and liberation are solid proof that this institution which ruled by Ulama, can provide numerous loyal followers if needed. How come these religious institutions have such powerful force on influencing its students? From *Manuver*

*Politik Ulama*, Komaruddin Hidayat and M. Yudhie Haryono (2004) explained that there are several conditions in understanding the vulnerability of Islamic institutions:

a.      Hierarchic Structure

One of many characteristic of Islamic society is their strong hierarchy and patrimonial culture. Religion in general presents fact that the values which exist in most society are not scribbled, but rather structured. Islam society is textual society; there are writings about structures in behaving, obedience towards Allah (God), prophet, leaders, and parents. These texts then interpreted according to local tradition; prophet and their family, major best friend, minor best friend, major follower, minor follower, Ulama, *Kiai*, *gus*, and so on. Through acculturation process in Java, where parents reside on top of the structure, Islamic culture also influenced and pesantren has hierarchic structure as well.

b.      Anti Critic and Less Dialogue

Because of the hierarchic structure, each social agent has unique position and resulting in less dialogue, because the dialogue process cannot be equally conducted. This happens because each position broaden their power, hegemony, and monopoly in the form of charismatic persona which are built to be inherited by their clan/successor (biological or not). So when the dialogue ideas are restrained, critics are also banned because they could damage Ulama's reputation.

c.      Afterlife Syndrome

To maintain the effectiveness of Ulama's dogma progress and their charisma, the curriculum of study which Ulama teach is not about worldly matter but instead the afterlife. Ritual of prayer is the most important parameter in judging the Islamic society, rather than the social parameter. This spiritual idea helps a lot of people to overcome their sadness, bad day, illness, and any suffering. This would make the santri vulnerable when the afterlife wisdom taught purposefully wrong or deviate from the original meaning.

d.      Romanticism

When afterlife syndrome getting acute, santri begin to use old terminology and conservative logic in solving their worldly problems. For example is how Prophet Muhammad era never considered as historical but rather his wisdom are very much alive in the daily life of the followers. His presence, even after thousands of years, still has strong impact in calming, resolving, and answering the matter of humanity for his followers. This is why, if Ulama deviate from their right path, all they have to do is preaching some modified Prophet's wisdom to the followers; the oblivious followers who suffers from this romanticism syndrome would not take a second look to the modern logic and eventually fall for the trap.

e.        Absolutism

The effect from romanticism is close-minded perspective the santri will have later on. Because of this perspective, santri cannot open themselves to the new improvements or ideas from foreign source in which resulting an absolutism dilemma. Hidayat and Haryono (2004, p.28) also included Karen Armstrong (2000) from his book *The Battle for God* which argues that religion absolutism operates with; (1) advising that *logos* (science) is not enough to understand the world. (2) Breeding myths; saviors or heroes myths, God's commandments myths, chosen civilization myths, crime myths, and liberation myths. (3) Introducing charismatic figures. (4) Presenting high degree *'sense of belonging.'* (5) Transmitting *'holiness or sacredness'* in worldly life. (6) Informing that Islam doctrine is the most absolute and never wrong.

Ulama charismatic persona and high influence, combined with educational institution with loyal followers, would considerably make them a perfect instrument for political or capital interest. Moreover, pesantren characteristics which are secluded and hierarchic in its structure are producing rather close-minded followers who devote themselves more to afterlife subject than worldly concern. Even though not all pesantren has traits like what described above, but in general pesantren with traditional values are dominant in Indonesia, usually located in villages far from the main cities.

***

## Kiai and Society

There are variation of terms to identify moslem scholar, in previous section, Ulama already introduced as *'legal scholars engaged in the several fields of Islamic studies who have completed several years of training and study of Islamic disciplines.'* Kiai, however, described as *'saints who are gifted'* by Turmudi (2003, p.1). As informal Islam leader, Kiai is also *'someone who is believed by the villagers to have high authority and charisma'.* This type of authority is categorized as *'outside the routine daily life'* as argued by Weber (1973), thus Kiai are perceived to have extraordinary gifts from God which make their leadership widely recognized. Besides their personal gifts, authority of Kiai and the close relationship with society are built by Kiai's devotion and their orientation to Islamic society's needs. This strategic position of Kiai then utilized by political parties, especially when these parties are intensely penetrated the society of Java.

Compared to other local elites, like rich farmer, Kiai, mostly who runs pesantren, has more respectable position. Kiai leadership ability can easily be used for gathering mass for social movements. There are two factors which are the main cause of Kiai's powerful position: (1) Kiai's knowledge and wisdom attracts villagers to learn from them and also make Kiai have a lot of followers. (2) Kiai usually comes from wealthy family, and Kiai's economic resources often make their followers dependent. Moreover, because of the wealth, Kiai can blend with important figure in society, thus securing their leadership power.

However, Turmudi research also mentioned about recent studies which shows that Kiai's position in society gradually shifted (Usman, 1991) along with their socio-political views (Abdullah, 1988) and consequently need new approach. Kiai role in Java villages, which were before very charismatic and significant, is now getting eroded. Kiai are not really apparent on local government projects in the village. Villagers now prefer to visit government officials in their village rather than Kiai. However Kiai still placed in the noteworthy position for Islamic society for these reasons: (1) Traditionally, Kiai are also elites who have influence over Islamic society, (2) Kiai are also elite politicians who have influence over Islamic society's political behavior. The dependableness of villagers towards Kiai might caused Kiai, if affected by outside influence (like political parties or capital business) abuse their power.

In general, Kiai and Ulama both has the power to mass influence the Islamic society, be it through academic institution like pesantren, or as village leader and important figure. Even though their intention towards the society is harmless, but people with capital or political interest can exploit and use them as tools for their sake. There is one method, the most efficient one which Ulama and Kiai used in order to spread and synchronize their visions to people; it is through Dakwah.

\*\*\*

## Dakwah

As one of the important method in gaining followers and harmonize visions from Kiai or Ulama to the society, *dakwah* cannot be left out as its importance is significant. Dr. Moh Ali Aziz (2002) on *Ilmu Dakwah* come up with three main points of dakwah:

a. Dakwah is a process of delivering the teachings of Islam from one person to another.
b. Dakwah can be about *amr ma'ruf* (teaching of the good) and *nahi mun'kar* (avoidance and prevention to the bad).
c. All above efforts are carried out deliberately in order to make Islamic society obey and act according to the Islam teachings.

From above points it is clear that the purpose of dakwah is to transmit teachings of Islam to the moslems, drive people to the right path of Islam and avoid the bad. In order to spread the teachings effectively, there are several media used in dakwah:

a. Spoken Words

Included in this category are each media which can be hear by ear, also known as *audible media* such as oral speech, presentation, training, or through audible device like phone, radio, and so on.

b. Printed Writings

Included in this category are printed items, printed pictures, paintings, books, newspapers, magazines, brochures, pamphlets, and so on.

c. Audio Visual

Included in this category are all above two categories combined; film, television, video, and so on.

d. Akhlak

*Akhlak* can be perceived as evident behavioral example (encourages the society to follow) which portrays Islamic teachings.

Besides the importance of media to transmit the teachings, there are also several approaches in Dakwah: (1) cultural approach, (2) academicals approach, (3) psychological approach. Cultural approach has been around Indonesia since a long time ago through acculturation, while academicals approach can be achieved through academic institutions which use Islamic teachings as the main root. Psychological approach tends to be more persuasive even though nothing coercive method used as it is irrelevant in Islamic teachings.

Dakwah will always have reaction from its audience. Aziz (2004, p.138) listed three Dakwah effects which are:

a. Cognitive Effect

After successfully received the message from dakwah, audience will absorb the contents through thinking process, and this cognitive effect could happen if there are changes which are different from what the audience usually believed about the dakwah contents.

b. Affective Effect

In this phase audience will decide through their process of understanding whether the message from dakwah is good enough to be admitted.

c. Behavioral Effect

Audience will behave according to the message transmitted through dakwah if they think that the dakwah is worth, through their observation, thinking, understanding, and decision.

## Moral Masochism

Moslem scholar become a politician in what they believed to be troubled regime like Indonesia usually triggered by what Simon Freud called *moral masochism* (Hidayat, Haryono; 2004, p.36). According to Freud, moral masochism is the awareness of having desires to be punished in non erotic way (which differs from other type of masochism), with a purpose to eliminate the guilt feeling. This becomes some kind of *defense of ego* to counter any guilt which arises from certain needs and moral masochism agent feels that they have to moralize other people too. Moral masochism operates through four phases: (1) misbehavior phase (wrong political behavior/preference); (2) guilty feeling (self guilt because of wrong political behavior/preference); (3) need for punishment (awareness to be punished to eliminate the guilt feeling); (4) forgiveness (feeling of ease because the need for punishment is fulfilled so society will forgive them and their relationship with society is fixed). After they gone through these four phases, they would let the people vote or leave the current competing candidates.

There are also four external factors which makes Moslem scholar emerge on the political arena (Hidayat, Haryono; p.39), such as: (1) civil politician's lack of confidence on themselves and their political party to construct and mold them as public leader; (2) political assurance in constitution level is fragile because no winning political party dominate the parliament; (3) parliament and extra-parliament control is getting stronger because political knowledge in society is also growing; (4) only small support are given to candidates by political party because of the multi-party system's consequences. Because of these factors, moslem scholar appear to be the ideal candidate to secure the fragile throne of power since they have charismatic figure and large amount of loyal followers. The weakness of parliament will be supported by extra-parliament power from Islamic organizations with real fanatical mass power.

The relation between moslem scholar and politician will always be repeated in every occasion, especially when democracy and politic fail to build political rationalism and secularization, thus making the metamorphose drama of moslem scholar becomes politician will always have effortless entrance. Relation between moslem scholar and politician can be seen on diagram (Hidayat, Haryono; p.40) below:

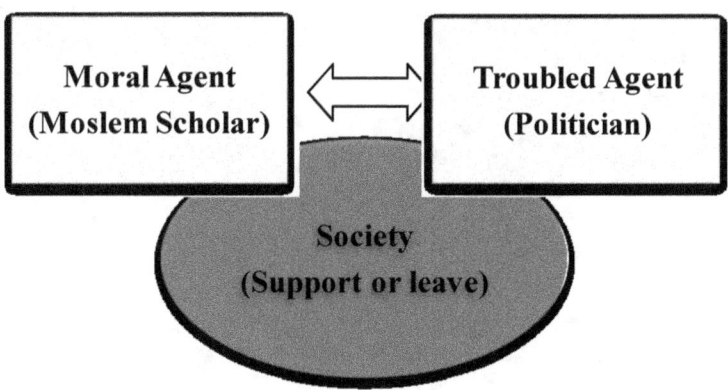

**Diagram 1** Relation, result and purpose of moslem scholar and politician coalition

For politician, moslem scholar and its followers will be used for *supporting, cleansing, clutching,* and *protecting* from critics and political threat from parliament and extra-parliament. While for moslem scholar, politician are agent who will have to be *tied, fixed, directed,* and *dominated.* In the end, the result of moslem scholar and politician coalition are only three: *trusted/voted, distrusted/left* and *ignored.* This shows that moslem scholar can be analogized as investor, with their followers as free stock, position as investment, and politic as stock market.

The next question arise is that how the followers or society would fall for their political scheme, be it coming from moslem scholar or politician. From *Menggugat Otoritas dan Tradisi Agama*, Abdul Karim Soroush (2000) stated that if honesty and virtue with all their terms and conditions are perceived as good even though there are still exceptions, then same thing also applies for fraudulence crime; maybe in general these behavior perceived as bad, but they are still relative, different people have different mind in asserting these phenomenon. The main reasons are:

a. People cannot decide whether virtue, like honesty, always good or bad. It seems that they have to wait until all universal terms and condition needed are found so the final decision about the good or bad can be made.

b. Time needed for someone to wait for the accumulative terms and condition or the method to achieve those are still not clear, or whether the method used is rational or experimental.

c. Even though all evidences, terms and conditions needed are already found, how can we tell that the good is actually good or the bad is bad since the methods itself are unclear.

d. All these requirements are only blurring and frustrate the judgment. Moral and ethic cannot be perceived only by the number of fulfilled terms or conditions.

e. In the end people go by their own definition in judging this moral and ethic issue.

Factors listed above are the reason people follow moslem scholar or politician without second thought. Too much thinking over this matter is confusing and frustrating, and as loyal followers they usually believe in their leader more than outsiders. Good or bad for them are what their leader chose, whatever the result, they will follow. This is also applies for political decision, whomever the leader support, their follower will also vote. Below is a diagram to describe more about moslem scholar and politician operates:

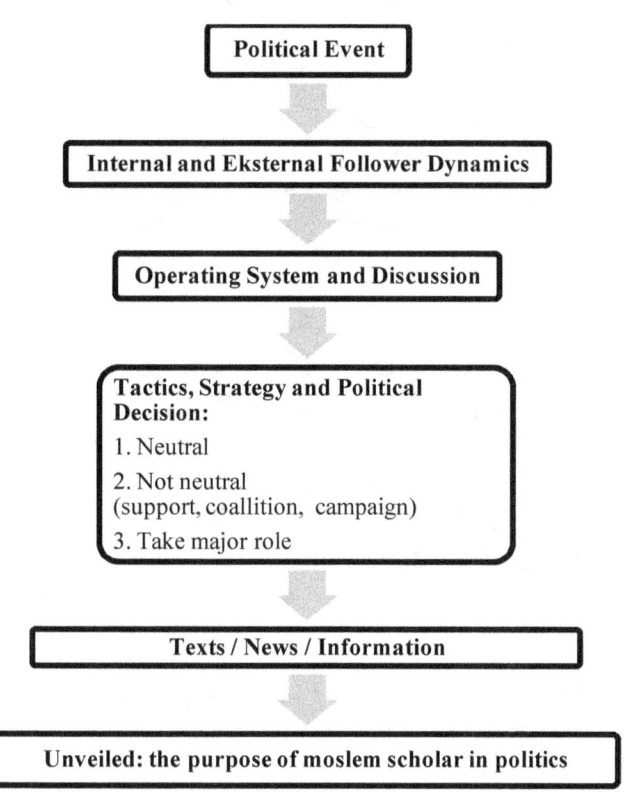

**Diagram 2** Moslem Scholar Political Operation (Hidayat, Haryono; p. 42)

After political event took place, there is internal and external dynamic in the follower side; this is where the reasoning of Soroush's about moral/ethic debate occurs. In such situation, the leader along with other moslem scholar and some of their follower discussed about their voice according to this matter, be it neutral or not. After they decided their political act, they let the public know through various media, thus their intention soon will be revealed to all.

\*\*\*

## Welfare

There are reasons as to why people can easily accept religious doctrines, despite the validation of its source. Indonesia, as third world developing country, has quite major issues in term of social welfare and the people have been exploited since the beginning of monarch and feudalism era. From *Islam di Indonesia*, Amien Rais (1986) listed three forms of people exploitation in Indonesia: (1) Unfair trade in selling goods, (2) Unfair payment in services provided and (3) High tax subjected to the people by the ruling government from feudal era.

This injustice has been going on for decades in Indonesia and produces a large amount of deprived mass without productive asset or any other asset which could create revenue. In the end, this deprived mass becomes overly dependable to the people who owns productive asset, and thus begin a *patron client* relationship, where the deprived mass becomes the sub-dominant class which entirely surrender themselves for the ruling class. Besides creating patron client relationship, eliminating the mass from productive asset also caused mass unemployment and idleness, which make dependency ratio between unproductive people and productive people are getting higher.

An example in another country, of how deprived mass could devote themselves in the religious doctrines can be found on Human Right Watch Asia (1997) with their book titled *China: State Control of Religion*. They wrote that in china, poverty increased the desire of the unfortunates to be wealthy, and fascinatingly this also in sync with their cultural beliefs which states that if one cannot be rich in real life then they still have a chance to be rich in the next life. This phenomenon is where religion took part, as quoted below:

> *"The hardship in religion is an expression of the hardship in real life; it is also a protest against that hardship. Religion is the sigh of the oppressed soul, the feeling of a heartless world, just like it is the spirit of spiritless system. Religion is the people's opium"*
>
> *– Karl Marx*

From the book Human Right Watch Asia further explained that Religion's ritual interested these poor people who have nothing enjoyable in their life. Poor and sick people have nowhere to go (because of their financial limitation) except plead to God to cure their disease as in their religious belief, illness is somehow connected with the "devil". So in order to cast away their plague caused by the devil, they seek help from religion.

Don Fitz (1996) from *Gateway Green Alliance*[3] reviewed the work of John Stauber and Sheldon Rampton's *Toxic Sludge Is Good for You: Lies, Damn Lies and the Public Relations Industry* which framed variety of social activists related with public relation industry, they are (1) *Radicals*, (2) *Opportunists*, (3) *Idealists*, and (4) *Realists*. However, social activist groups are not only limited to the media and its relatives, at religious extent, there are also activist groups with the same traits trying to squeeze themselves in the society. Based on Stauber and Sheldon Rampton's typology, religious groups can also be categorized with the significance of such traits, but in this case, there are only two categories matches with Indonesian religious groups: *Radicals* and *Opportunists*. However, there are also a type of Islamic religious group which are usually be on target from the other two; the *Liberalists*. Idealist and Realist view are not necessarily relevant in Indonesia's case of religious group typology, so this book will only categorizing the major three.

***

## The Radical

One of the data collected by John Stauber and Sheldon Rampton (1991) reveals that radical activists *'want to change the system and have underlying socio/political motives'* and perceive

---

[3] http://www.greens.org/s-r/11/11-23.html

multinational corporations as *'inherently evil.'* These organizations do not trust the federal state and local governments to guard them and to preserve the environment. They believe that individuals and local groups should have direct authority over industry. In Indonesia case, a lot of religious groups, specifically Islamic groups, fall to this category. Several factors that might differentiate them from each other are the use of physical force in their coercive method of *'revolution'* and their respect of Indonesia's constitution in the form of obeying the law and respecting the human rights and social norms. According to an article written by Lutfi Bashori[4] (2009), there are two types of radical Islamic groups: ideologically radical and ideologically & behaviorally radical. The first category is groups who have their own radical views but they are limiting their behavior, not in any form of their actions are clashing with the law and social norms. These groups usually voiced their thoughts on media (including social media on the internet), public debates, *dakwah*, and many publications (they write journals, books, articles, etc). Unlike the ideologically radical groups, there are also exists groups which are radical in both ideology and behavior; they use physical force and go against the law, often terrorizing the society.

*** 

## Ideologically Radical

There are several groups which belong to this category; most of them prefer staying low and blend in the society, not looking for trouble. Others are in the form of student organization; spreading their beliefs in many Universities. Despite their rather *mild* (in comparison to the other type of radical groups) approach in voicing their views, their Ideology is still to be considered radical. Agus Akhmadi on *Pengembangan Pemahaman Agama Yang Toleran* listed several groups:

a.        Jama'ah Tarbiyah

Jama'ah Tarbiyah is the inspiration of student Islamic political and ideological movement in the name of *Kesatuan Aksi Mahasiswa Muslim Indonesia* (KAMMI). Jama'ah Tarbiyah and KAMMI are amongst the groups which are easy to identify as they usually wear recognizable symbols and slogans on their clothes, bags, books, motorcycles, cars, or any places where they carry out their activities. This group exists in both private and state universities. They are often recruiting new members and place them in various intra-university student organizations to expand their movements. Tarbiyah movement was born from the dissatisfaction of other Islamic movement which considered accommodative to various things that are confronting with their ideal, such as what Muhammadiyah and NU usually act. However, they are also against Darul Islam / Tentara Islam Indonesia (DI/TII) action model (illegal and banned organization, revolting against Indonesia government in the past). Tarbiyah claimed themselves as new alternative of perfection.

---

[4] http://www.ppalanwar.com/index.php?mact=News,cntnt01,print,0&cntnt01articleid=122

b.      Forum Studi Islam (FOSI)

Forum Studi Islam (FOSI) is a study forum which prefers to be unexposed. Their members come from university students, along with the help of alumni and seniors, deepen their general Islamic knowledge and practical Islamic knowledge intensively to be carry out in their daily live. FOSI is not as progressive as Tarbiyah, but their doctrines and understandings are similar.

c.      Jamaah Tabligh

Different from Jamaah Tarbiyah and FOSI which main activity focused on universities, Jamaah Tabligh mostly active outside universities, even though their members mostly are university alumni. Tabligh followers mostly seen in group wearing white *gamis* clothes or simple *koko* clothes with turban on their head, along with trousers just above the ankle, and lastly; growing beard but no mustache. Most of the members are men because in their doctrines, women are supposed to be working at home as housewives.

d.      Jamaah Salafi

They are a group of people with sole purpose of doing Prophet Muhammad teachings and *Salaf Ulama* which are the Prophet *Sahabat* (generation after Prophet Muhammad), *Tabi'in* (Generation after *Sahabat*), and *Tabi'i-at-tabi'in* (Generation after *Tabi'in*). Jamaah Salafi believes that Islam taught by *Salaf Ulama* is the only authentic one because the time span of their teachings is closest to Prophet Muhammad. Similar to Tabligh's preference of outfit, they are also wear *gamis,* turban, white shirt or *koko,* ankle-length trousers, and growing beards. Even though Salafi and Tabligh have common religious behavior, their rituals are different.

e.      Hizbut Tahrir

Hizbut Tahrir does not solely exist in Indonesia, they are international organization with multiple bases around the world. According to their official website[5], *"Hizb ut-Tahrir is a political party whose ideology is Islam. Its objective is to resume the Islamic way of life by establishing an Islamic State that executes the systems of Islam and carries its call to the world. Hizb ut-Tahrir has prepared a party culture that includes a host of Islamic rules about life's matters. The party calls for Islam in its quality as an intellectual leadership from which emanates the systems that deals with all man's problems, political, economic, cultural and social among others. Hizb ut-Tahrir is a political party that admits to its membership men and women, and calls all people to Islam and to adopt its concepts and systems. It views people according to the viewpoint of Islam no matter how diverse their nationalities and their schools of thought were. Hizb ut-Tahrir adopts the interaction with the Ummah in order to reach its objective and it struggles against colonialism in all its forms and attributes in order to liberate the Ummah from its intellectual leadership and to deracinate its cultural, political, military and economic roots from the soil of the Islamic lands. Hizb ut-Tahrir endeavours to change the erroneous thoughts which colonialism has propagated, such as confining Islam to rituals and morals."* In Indonesia, Hizbut Tahrir religious activity does not emerge much on the surface; not many people

---

[5] http://english.hizbuttahrir.org/

aware of their existence. Hizbut Tahrir activists always insist the importance of staying low profile in society. They learned the misfortune occurred to activists from Middle East and prefer to avoid publications. Even though their ideology is radical, and they are against the state and government, they do not engage in any vandalism activity.

f.      Majelis Rasulullah

According to their official website[6] Majelis (council) Rasulullah is a council lead by Habib Munzir bin Fuad Al Musawa. Founded in 1998, this council frequently holds *pengajian* in Tuesday night at Al Munawar Mosque, Pancoran, South Jakarta. Habib Munzir's teachings focused on engaging moslems to *taubat* (repentance) and loving Prophet Muhammad and his *sunnah,* also making him an Idol for moslem. Majelis Rasulullah promotes 'Save Driving Movement' where members who has motorcycle wear black jacket and white *peci* (cap), but now switched to proper helmet.

g.      Majelis Nurul Musthofa

Majelis (council) Nurul Musthofa, according to their official website[7], was built on the year of 2000 to get closer to Allah and Rasulullah (Prophet Muhammad), lead by Habib Hassan Bin Jafar Assegaf. Before they are officially registered by Indonesia Religious Ministry, they held their activities from house to house, mosque to mosque. They gain their popularity on 2006, from 50 Mosques to 250 Mosques under their influence.

***

## Behaviorally Radical

Religious groups which fall to this category are mostly on the public and media spotlight for their anarchy, vigilante and vandalism. They do not hesitate flaunting their organization or religious symbols, and usually fiercer in voicing their doctrines than the ideologically radical ones. Besides spreading Islamic teachings though debate or *dakwah*, they are also believe that practical action is also needed in order to fix the behavior which they consider against or deviate from the way of Islam. Some of them through *softer* field action like demonstration, some of them into more destructive attempt. However in Indonesia, major radical groups, despite how vigilant their actions might be, the government cannot do much, let alone disband them.

---

[6] http://majelisrasulullah.org/index.php?option=com_content&task=view&id=2&Itemid=26

[7] http://www.nurulmusthofa.org/tentang-kami.html

a.      Forum Umat Islam (FUI)

Forum Umat Islam is frequently called as the father organization of various Islamic radical groups because multiple major organizations such as *Front Pembela Islam* (FPI), *Gerakan Reformasi* Islam (GARIS), *Majelis Mujahidin Indonesia* (MMI) are connected with them. SETARA Institute team (2010) on their book *The Faces of ISLAM Defenders; Religion Radicalism and Its Implications on Assurance of Religious/Beliefs Freedom in Jabodetabek and West Java* describe them as active in carrying out intolerant actions against Ahmadiyah and Jaringan Islam Liberal (Islamic Liberal Network). Although it was freshly founded, but within five years, FUI is swiftly growing in scores of areas in Indonesia and now it has 15 branches, among others are South Sulawesi, South Sumatra, North Sumatra, South Kalimantan, etc. even though they didn't do much field action, they are quite fierce on their activity, like when Mass Religious Meeting of FUI on 5 August, where they not only assailed Ahmadiyah and Islamic Liberal group but also intended to attack Islamic Liberal Network (JIL) office in Utan Kayu, East Jakarta. Half of the Meeting participants were already reached Salemba area on their way to Utan Kayu when they finally cancelled the plan because the office was guarded by hundreds of police and outnumbered them.

b.      Front Pembela Islam (FPI)

FPI is well known as the biggest Islamic radical mass organization, led by Habib Rizieq Syihab with branches in 28 provinces and claimed to have four million members. Most probably because of their violence in performing the raid of anti-immoral and Ahmadiyah, the actions of FPI have always drawn mass media and public attention. According to SETARA Institute team (2010) FPI mission is to perform *amar ma'ruf nahi mungkar* or spread the righteousness and prevent injustice according to Islam. The reason is because the widespread of immorality like prostitution, gambling and alcohol in Jakarta; all of which are considered harmful to the moral and *aqidah* of the Muslims. However, the law enforcement after reformation is weak and incapable to handle those immoralities. Thus, FPI was founded as the anti-immoral organization that tries to take over the authority of legal officers in maintaining order. Example of their action was when they attacked Ahmadiyah complex and restaurants, as quoted from Jakarta Globe[8] (2011): *"Police in the South Sulawesi capital have named the head of the armed wing of the hard-line Islamic Defenders Front a suspect in an attack on Sunday against the beleaguered Ahmadiyah sect. In the attack, the LPI, a unit of the Islamic Defenders Front (FPI), smashed several windows at the JAI complex, including at its mosque, and damaged a car and a motorcycle parked in the compound."*

c.      Gerakan Reformasi Islam (GARIS)

Founded by H. Chep Hernawan, GARIS is the radical Islamic mass organization made in Cianjur. Their branches widespread in some cities in West Java, like Bandung, Garut, Sukabumi etc, and they claimed to have thousands of members; 28 thousands members in Cianjur and 5 thousands in Sukabumi. A lot of aggression conducted by this organization had raised their name as one of radical groups in West Java. The last action was on 4th December 2010, when they dispersed the National Workshop (Mukernas) of

---

[8] http://www.thejakartaglobe.com/home/fpi-attacks-ahmadiyah-complex-and-restaurants/459311

Ahmadiyah in Hotel Setia, Cipanas, Cianjur. Before that, on 19 September 2005, hundreds of people from GARIS attacked four villages of Ahmadiyah sect in Cianjur; Panyairan, Cicakra, Neglasari and Ciparay. Around 43 houses, four mosques, three *madrasah* (Islamic school), five stalls and stores were destroyed including the chicken stall.

d.      Forum Ukhuwah Islamiyah (FUI)

Taken from SETARA (2010) interview, FUI is described as: *"a radical mass organization that frequently belabors immoral places, seals churches and also disbands heretical sects. These acts against everything which are considered as ignorance things are only strategies to accomplish the real FUI aspiration, which is upholding Islamic Shariah in Indonesia".* FUI became a significant Islamic mass organization in Cirebon for their numerous actions on the street. Gambling houses smashed, street prostitutes' raid. However, the act that lifted this radical mass organization name was the assault to the largest gambling games machine center in Cirebon at Jalan Pasuketan 18 on May 2005; FUI crowd sealed the location and destroyed various gambling machines.

e.      Tholiban

Tholiban is a radical organization from Tasikmalaya, they have conducted various anti-immoral actions such as gambling and prostitution sweeping which resulted in their increased fame and people's attention. Tholiban was born from the concern over immorality rampant in post-reform era (1998) on Tasikmalaya. Tholiban leader is Ajengan Zenzen from Al-Irsyadiyah *Pesantren* Tasikmalaya who is also good in politics. They have around 3000 members and mostly come from Miftahul Huda *pesantren*. The difference of this group from others is that they are not anti Ahmadiyah, in contrast to FPI, almost no case of attack against Ahmadiyah committed by Tholiban.

***

**The Opportunist**

Before listing the possible candidates of opportunists group, we better engulf ourselves on the definitions of opportunism and correlate those to the religious groups, finding their visible traits and area where they are usually exploit the opportunities every now and then. The radical groups, especially, are considered to have opportunist side since religion is just instrument for funding their organizations. Because in Indonesia's religious groups case, what apparent on the outside might not be a representation of what is going on inside.

Michael Dietrich (1994) on *Transaction Cost Economics and beyond: towards a New Economics of the Firm* explained about opportunism from economic view based on Williamson (1985) definition as:

*"The incomplete or distorted disclosure of information, especially to calculated efforts to mislead, distorts, disguise, obfuscate, or otherwise confuse. It is responsible for real or contrived conditions of information asymmetry, which vastly complicate problems of economic organization."*

While on political side, Ard Schilder (2000) on his book *Government Failures and Institutions in Public Policy Evaluation: The Case of Dutch Technology Policy* he argued that political opportunism is related to the relation between politicians and voters. Quoting Hermes and Schilder (1998) he added:

*"Political opportunism may be defined as the short-term manipulation of economic or political variables to secure re-election."*

Examples are the manipulation of economic indicators (unemployment) or the possibility of granting privileges to groups that can help to gain majority with elections. However, in general, opportunism manifest itself in various ways, such as lying, stealing, cheating, calculated efforts to mislead, distorts, disguise, obfuscate, or otherwise confuse; as stated in *Responsible Marketing: Concepts, Theories, Models, Strategies and Cases* by Oswald A.J. Mascarenhas (2007).

In correlation with religious groups, there are some of them which apparently matches the criteria of opportunistic behavior on several definitions above; they have tendencies to lie, steal, cheat, calculate their efforts to mislead, distorts, disguise, obfuscate, or confuse their followers or society. Usually in economically advance countries, religious organizations no longer have much political power, though they may still be an essential social force; the leaders of religious groups can be influential in social and, to a degree, political life, but the allegiance of the believers is hardly ever expressed by straight and vigorous action in the political ground, as stated by Edward Luttwak (1979) from *Coup D'État: A Practical Handbook*. Meanwhile for economically developing countries and those whose development is limited or even backwards, the situation is otherwise; God is the most supreme importance. This can be a foundation of very substantial political power to the organizations which are identified with proper beliefs and able to channel the sentiments of the believers.

## Funding

Moving on to the Religious Opportunist Group in Indonesia, one indicator that can be very well in measuring their opportunism traits is fund; how they are funding their action and where is the source. SETARA Institute team (2010) has some good examples based on their research concerning the radical groups in Indonesia, GARIS case for example; almost their entire operational fund is financed from personal assets of H Chep Hernawan and his family. It is possible because this head of GARIS is a successful entrepreneur in Garut. He has businesses in plastic bags, property and also Cianjur rice distribution. Tithe and *infaq* (charity) from his family are often used for GARIS' activity. However besides the leader's asset, they are also gathered a lot of funds from their member and charity action (GARIS members went to the street holding charity boxes). They are also reported by Aljazeera news media (as quoted by Tempo Interaktif[9] news media) to have Lieutenant General (retiree) of Indonesian military funded them in order to have a revolt against the current President, Susilo Bambang Yudhoyono, by creating havoc towards Ahmadiyah sect in Cikeusik, Banten.

On the other side, FPI frequently accepts donation from outsiders to finance their demonstration; in front of American Embassy Jakarta at October 2001, for two days FPI masses protested against America's strike to Afghanistan. FPI admitted that their action was also financed by outside FPI who approved this agenda. Other than donations, they have several financial institutions in the form of *Baitul Mal* or in Arabic term translated as "House of money" or "House of Wealth." Historically, it was a financial institution responsible for the administration of taxes in Islamic states. One of them located at Pancoran Mas Depok, called BTM (Baitul Mal) Al Kautsar. Branches are required to get contribution fee from their members as low as Rp 1000 each month per member. However from Wikileaks outburst recently, it was revealed that FPI might receive funds from Indonesia's national police. Pedomannews.com[10], an online news media wrote that Yahya Assegaf, BIN (*Badan Intelijen Negara* or Nation's Intelligence Division) senior officer stated that the current Indonesia police chief Susanto considered FPI as their '*attack dog.*' On Wikileaks telegram, reported that FPI was used by the police to attack United States Embassy Jakarta on February 2006. Further stated on Pedomannews.com article, the police utilized FPI as '*attack* dog' so people would not blame police anymore on human rights infringement. From Tempo[11], a reputable news media, an article published on their website about FPI not denying the Wikileaks revelation about them being Police's right hand men. FPI representative Muharman further claimed that if they are said to be Police's right hand men, then it is only for the sake of virtue towards society.

Besides the relation between FPI and police, there is also a published article about FPI leader, Habib Rizieq, declared his support to President and Vice President of Indonesia

---

[9] http://www.tempo.co/read/news/2011/03/23/078322228/Ngabalin-Bantah-Ikut-Dewan-Revolusi-Islam

[10] http://www.pedomannews.com/politik-hukum-dan-keamanan/10753-polisi-dan-bin-danai-fpi

[11] http://www.tempo.co/read/news/2011/09/04/078354550/Munarman--Yahya-Assegaf-Antek-Amerika

candidates on 2009 election: Jusuf Kalla and Wiranto. Below is the translated news from Okezone[12] News, an online news portal:

> *"We encourage all FPI members inside or outside Indonesia, and all the people to vote for JK (Jusuf Kalla) – Wiranto"* – Sobri Lupis, FPI Secretary-General.

> *"Support to JK-Wiranto given due to both political leaders are proven to have commitment in maintaining the field of Religion. They are committed to eliminate all forms of blasphemy and defamation of Religion. One of them is the case of Ahmadiyah sect."*

Other than the obvious and major names of radical groups, there are also exist Islamic council which are frequently holding a study or reciting activity in Islamic teachings, such as *Majelis Rasulullah* (Rasulullah Council) and *Majelis Nurul Musthofa* (Nurul Musthofa Council). The leader is called *Habib*, which is the identity name of someone who is a descendant of Prophet Muhammad. They are not considered behaviorally or ideologically radical, as they are often claimed by others with different view as misguided and deviate from general Islamic teachings, however their financial growth are so impressive, and from several media coverage, funds are not only coming from internal source, but also external. Merdeka.com[13], an online news media interviewed Ismail Fajrie Alatas, a historian live in Jeruk Purut, Jakarta and also doctoral candidate in University of Michigan USA. Below is the translation of the original article written in Bahasa Indonesia published on 2nd March 2012:

- **In your opinion, does Habib has affiliation to political party?**

"I think they are not total into politics, bringing these councils into political sphere. But as individual, they still have their rights to involve in politics. It's just their ways, for example Habib Mundzir, on the election of Jakarta governor last time. One of the candidates is Fauzi Bowo, known by Nahdhatul Ulama, close with Habaib, close with Ulama, recite Al-Qur'an since childhood in Kwitang. Another candidate, Adang Darajatun, carried out by *Partai Keadilan Sejahtera* (PKS). Mundzir (Habib of Majelis Rasulullah) could not say 'go vote' (to his followers). (But instead) Mundzir said, 'if you want to vote for a governor, vote the one who love *maulid* (celebrating the birth of

---

[12] http://news.okezone.com/read/2009/06/26/268/233251/fpi-deklarasi-dukung-jk-wiranto

[13] http://www.merdeka.com/khas/ismail-fajrie-alatas-1-Habib-dan-Kiai-juga-butuh-duit.html

Prophet Muhammad), don't vote someone who doesn't love doing *maulid*. That was a big cue, even though his brother is high authority of PKS."

- **Are there indications of Habaib approaching the authorities for a specific interest?**

"Yes, it might. Now, for example, they (Habaib) were instructed to taught like that, then where did they get the money? Right? Like there is even any *wakaf* (donation) from the state to those *Ustadz* or Habib? None. For that reason, they have to look for a job. This is to help the monetary. For example, to revive the council: selling posters, calendars, jackets, CDs. This is also helping the financial".

- **How about logrolling?**

"I don't know whether these two councils (Majelis Rasulullah and Nurul Musthofa) exist or not. However, what I know, the big *Kiai*, big Habib, whose masses are large are always like that. Maybe logrolling, but not too explicit. But that means the politicians must be giving money for this. Because they (the Habib) have to manage their people. This is patronage relationship. They (Habib) also need money to build *maulid* council. Feeding that much people, where does the money come from? Of course from politicians, big authorities. Politician and big authority can sit together in capital stage. This is symbiotic mutualism, benefitting each other. Politician needs visibility from Habaib. But for that visibility they need money. For example, to grill their lamb and so on".

- **Do you see Majelis Taklim (Islamic Study Council) in Jakarta already used for political vehicle? In example when Jusuf Kalla visited Majelis Rasulullah and President at Nurul Musthofa.**

"Not as explicit as that. If JK (Jusuf Kalla) come to MR (majelis Rasulullah), and SBY went to NM (Nurul Musthofa), that was everyone's rights to come. They are public councils. If come as head of country or minister, they will get their time to speak. It is a part of *ulil amri* (obeying the leader of moslem society). Everyone who come will be served. I think Mundzir and Hasan are not interested in using their council for political interest. However political choice is common. For example, Mundzir chose the governor who like maulid, it is a matter of preference".

According to the interview, about Jakarta Governor Fauzi Bowo and Indonesia President Susilo Bambang Yudhoyono visitation to Majelis Rasulullah, an article regarding that matter was also published by verified online news media Tempo on February 5th 2012. Below are the translated portions from the said article:

> *"This morning, February 5th 2012, President Susilo Bambang Yudhoyono also attending the zikir akbar (mass prayer in Islamic teachings) whose held by Majelis Rasulullah on Monas, Central Jakarta."*

*"Furthermore spotted his youngest son Edhie Baskoro Yudhoyono, Secretary of State Minister Sudi Silalahi, Minister of Religion Suryadharma Ali, Jakarta Governor Fauzi Bowo, and other party as well. Some foreign ambassadors from major Islamic Countries like Saudi Arabia, Yemen, and Libya are also attending"*

\*\*\*

## Membership

Another indicator of a possible opportunistic trait of organization or group is how they recruit their members. Based on previous segment, it is evident that funds plays a vital part on organization's existence and from several news coverage, symbiotic relationship between religious group and politicians frequently happens for the sake of money. Organization with mass members usually accused of being opportunist, especially since the group's executives usually getting wealthier along with the increase of the member's growth. J. Richard Harrison and Glenn Carroll (2006) on *Culture and Demography in Organization* quoting Endlich (1999) about Goldman Sachs (an investment bank) case in recruitment process:

*"It begins in the recruitment process, long before a formal offer is extended. Brains are not enough. The first couple of interviews determine whether a candidate meets the firm's intellectual standards; the remainder, where far more candidates stumble, are used to determine "fit." It is a grueling process that tests endurance as well as aptitude. Those candidates who do not evince a scorching ambition, total commitment, and an inclination for teamwork are quickly weeded out."*

For company as noteworthy as Goldman Sachs, finding the perfect employee by building the high standards on the recruitment process is only natural, but how about other organizations? Of course rationally, they will look for the best available too. However, do these values also apply to opportunist organizations? Or their recruitment is far simpler? SETARA Institute (2010) explains about some radical religious groups' recruitment for membership. Apparently there are similarities between radical organization in recruiting members, particularly the ones which have individual membership such as FPI, GARIS, etc. Basically, the recruiting process is fairly loose, everyone can become member and the procedures are also simple; the person only needs to join *pengajian* (Al-Quran recitation) which are held by the organizations several times, then they can become member.

FPI, for example, if one interested in joining this organization, all they have to do is attending the events held by FPI such as *pengajian* lead by Habib Rizieq at Jami Al Islah Mosque, Petamburan, every Wednesday. They can also come to *pengajian* in Habib Rizieq's residence every Thursday night. Once they succeeded to meet all requirements, the can ask for recommendation from other committee member of FPI so they can finally become members. The case of Topik Hidayat's recruitment, for example, he is a member from Cempaka Putih, an elementary school graduate. Topik admitted that he become FPI member after following three *pengajian* held by Habib Rizieq in Al Islah Mosque. However, FPI occasionally recruits member with formal procedure, like open recruitment; where they spread forms around mosques and *Majelis Ta'lim*. Applicants are given several tests like reciting Al Quran verses, interviews about basic Islamic knowledge such as: Islamic essential principle (*rukun Islam*), faith essential principle (*rukun iman*), and *syahadat* (the declaration if one wants to embrace the religion of Islam). However these formal recruitment procedures only occurred occasionally; once or two times a year or doesn't occur at all.

Being a member of these organizations is easy, so does the resignation; they don't have to tell the committee and can resign anytime without penalty. Person who does not active in the organization activity are no longer considered as a member. Besides attending *pengajian* like FPI and other organization or *majelis*, organizations which mass base is *pesantren* can consider their *santri* (students) as members automatically. However, this membership recruitment triggers my curiosity; its simplicity, the quantity over quality while they are not even political parties. Correlating these facts to their funds, and how the leaders are getting wealthier, one does not simply missed the hint of a possible exploitation towards the clueless members, be it financial or political, as published in Gatra.com[14] news media about the contrast of how Habib Hasan (Majelis Nurul Mustofa) wealth before the organization fame and after the fame:

> "... 'Since he started to have his own home,' he said. Before that, Hasan lived nomadic on some rich Habib lover pilgrims."

***

## The Liberal

Sartika Soesilowati on *Perkembangan Model, Order Perdamaian, dan Keamanan Internasional* explained the focus of liberal group in maintaining institution, birth of the world government,

---

[14] http://www.gatra.com/hukum/31-hukum/8755-qkami-disuruh-mijitinq

networking, and cooperation. While Hussin Mutalib (2008) on *Islam in Southeast Asia* described Islam Liberal espouses a liberal interpretation of the *syari'ah* in confronting issues of modernity. In Indonesia, this particular Islamic practice tends to occupy quite a bit of media space, including the internet. Radical and opportunists groups are mostly go against them. Liberal Islam group in Indonesia usually very tolerable towards religious diversity and defend other religions when they are discriminated or attacked by either government or radical groups.

In Indonesia, the most famous Liberal Islam group is JIL, which stands for *Jaringan Islam Liberal* or Liberal Islam Network. According to their official website[15], their views of Liberal Islam are: (1) *Opens the door of Ijtihad (rational interpretation Islamic texts)*, (2) *prioritizing the spirit of religious-ethics, not the literal meaning of the texts*, (3) *believe in the open, plural relativity of truth*, (4) *favor the minorities and oppressed*, (5) *believe in the freedom of religion*, and (6) *separate the worldly authority with hereafter and religious authority with politics*. Their missions include:

1. Develop liberal interpretation of Islam in accordance with the principle JIL profess, and pass it to the widest possible audience.
2. Try to open a space for dialogue which is pressure-free from the conservatism. JIL are confident that the opening of dialogue's space will bloom a healthy Islamic thoughts and movement.
3. Pursue the creation of fair and humane social and political structure.

JIL thoughts and movements are widely and famously published in several noteworthy media, be it printed or digital. Their tolerance towards minorities also seizes the attention from international community.


\*\*\*


## The Difference

After explaining the typology of religious group in Indonesia which are *radical*, *opportunist*, and *liberalist*, we can clearly see the some opportunist groups are also exist in radical category. But does all radicals considered opportunist? There are distinctions and similarities which differentiate behaviorally radicals, opportunists, and the others, as listed before: *funds* and *membership*. Based on those two traits, this book considers the following (see table):

| Other Types | Opportunists | Behaviorally Radicals |
|---|---|---|
| Some of them think that money is worldly matter and | Tendencies to raise funds as much as possible through | Tendencies to raise funds as much as possible through |

---

15 http://islamlib.com/id/halaman/tentang-jil

| | | |
|---|---|---|
| clashing with their fundamental beliefs, thus funding is not their main priority. Some others might do well in financial but not acquired through deception. | deception, even building a financial institution to gather money and affiliating secretly with politicians, one of organization's leader is proven wealthier. | deception, even building a financial institution to gather money and affiliating secretly with politicians. |
| Not (or not yet seen) involved with politicians or proclaim that they support certain politician. | Involved with politicians, even proclaiming their support to presidential candidate. | Involved with politicians, especially if they have the same ideas regarding certain matters (i.e. Ahmadiyah Sect) |
| Usually have fewer members than the opposing two, and recruitment is tighter, since some of them valued the fundamental thinking of Islam, and some other chose to be more secular; not everyone have what they need. | Mass member, quantity over quality, this is also correlate to their funding. More members mean more financial and political assets. | Mass member, quantity over quality, this is also correlate to their funding, especially they are frequently marching the streets, doing raids, and sweeping. |
| Some of them appears a lot on the media (due to their thoughts or publications), but mostly are not because they never do anything destructive. | Appears a lot, especially if they "advertise" some politicians or just to "show" the public that they are a good friends so it will influence public political behavior; Be it through march or banner on the street. | Appears a lot, since they are doing destructive act towards the society. |

**Table 1** Differentiation between Religious Groups

From the table above, there are two groups which traits are similar; *opportunist* and *behaviorally radical*. However, it does not automatically means that all behaviorally radical groups are also opportunist, the conclusion only limited to the groups mentioned on this book. Associating with the previous chapter about cultural background in Indonesia, regarding how *Ulama* and *Kiai* plays integral part in the history of Islam here, then we can clearly see why most religious group leaders are also *Ulama* or *Kiai*. The only difference would be whether they are *Habib* or not. With their charismatic aura and long history of cultural background about how moslem society perceived them, if some opportunistic individuals want to gain financial or political assets, they can try identify themselves with *Ulama* or *Kiai* image and tricked the oblivious victim. Religion in this matter does not their only concern and in matter of fact, religion might perceived by them as a mere tool towards their ambition. Despite their attempt to use religion as an instrument, keep in mind that they are *also* a tool used by others whose power are far higher above them.

## Understanding The Concept from Postmodern Paradigm

Recent news and criminal cases have shown that there is a possibility which these religious groups are not really convey their 'religious' part, but instead they merely opportunists employ the sacred and popular terms of 'religion' as their identity. In *Theoretical Criminology*, (George Bryan Vold, Thomas J. Bernard, Jeffrey B. Snipes; 2002) there is an explanation of postmodern approach which examines *the relationship between human agency and language in creating meaning, identity, truth, justice, power, and knowledge.* This relationship is studied through 'discourse analysis,' a method of investigating how sense and meaning are constructed in which attention is paid to the values and assumptions implied in language. Discourse analysis considers *the social position of the person who is speaking or writing in order to understand the meaning of what is said or written*, not an analysis of the social roles that people occupy. Rather, it considers *how language is embedded in these roles and how that language shapes and forms the way people in these roles think and speak*, also known as 'discursive subject positions.' once people assume one of these 'discursive subject positions,' then *the words that they speak no longer fully express their realities, but to some extent express the realities of the larger institutions and organizations.* So how we analyze this 'Religious Opportunist Group' through this postmodern paradigm? First, is to learn their *language* of the *role* they are *playing*.

\*\*\*

## The Not-So-Religious Leader

They established themselves under a religious flag; in this case, Islam. They are also held many activities according to Islamic teachings, such as *Pengajian* (reciting Al-Qur'an verses) and *Dakwah* (spreading Islamic teachings). Not to mention the male members (and also the Habibs) are *uniforming* themselves with *ideal Islamic pilgrims* appearance: white *gamis* clothes or simple *koko* clothes with turban (mostly the leader, members usually wear simple *peci* or cap) on their head, along with trousers just above the ankle, and lastly; growing beard but no mustache. These groups, identifying themselves with Islamic fashion because they are expected to; by the society no less. In Indonesia, people are mostly label the style mentioned before associated to Islam. This phenomenon explained in *Symbolic Interactionism* theory, where from *Sociology: Understanding a Diverse Society* by Margaret L. Andersen, Howard Francis Taylor (2007) analyzes society by addressing the subjective meanings that people impose on objects, events, and behaviors. According to symbolic interactionists, people behave based on what they believe, not just on what is objectively true. Thus, society is considered to be *socially constructed* through human interpretation. People interpret one another's behavior and these interpretations form social bonds. For example: a man wearing turban, growing beards, and wear *gamis* are automatically a faithful high-ranked Muslim Scholar. However, are they? Not every Ulama, Kiai, or even Habib chose to identify themselves using those attributes; some prefer wearing more moderate clothing. But this reality is happening now in Indonesia, all they have to do is appear according to what society expects, and people will believe.

Now from symbolic interactionism in Indonesia we already know how religious symbols could change people's perception towards the person who uses it, so if an organization frequently holding Islamic activities, flaunting Islamic symbols to the public, and the leader wearing moslem fashion, then people who seek for religious enlightenment would follow that organization. However what if their religiosity is only a façade? We already understand their language, and now let's move on to the effect of *how that language shapes and forms the way people in these roles think and speak.*

***

## Deception through Religious Symbolisms

Mentioned before in the religious group typology that some of them are caught interacting with politicians, and some of them growing their financial assets through various means such as members' contribution fees, charities, building financial institution, and possible political deals. However, the part which irked the most is that Habib, along with their organizations' financial growth, are also growing their financial wealth. Quoted below is a portion of news from Gatra.com, an online news media about Habib Hasan, Majelis Nurul Mustofa leader:

> "… 'Since he started to have his own home,' he said. Before that, Hasan lived nomadic on some rich Habib lover pilgrims."

There were also news about some of the groups, them affiliating with politicians, even police, for funding their organizations. Below are portions from news media (already written in previous segments and footnoted) about religious group involvement with politics:

> "… *GARIS* to have Lieutenant General (retiree) of Indonesian military funded them in order to have a revolt against the current President, Susilo Bambang Yudhoyono, by creating havoc towards Ahmadiyah sect in Cikeusik, Banten…" (Tempo Interaktif)

*"... Reported that FPI was used by the police to attack United States Embassy Jakarta on February 2006. The police utilized FPI as 'attack dog' so people would not blame police anymore on human rights infringement..." (Pedoman News)*

*"...FPI representative Muharman further claimed that if they are said to be Police's right hand men, then it is only for the sake of virtue towards society..." (Tempo Interaktif)*

*"We encourage all FPI members inside or outside Indonesia, and all the people to vote for JK (Jusuf Kalla) – Wiranto" – Sobri Lupis, FPI Secretary-General (Okezone News)*

*"I don't know whether these two councils (Majelis Rasulullah and Nurul Musthofa) exist or not. However, what I know, the big Kiai, big Habib, whose masses are large are always like that. Maybe logrolling, but not too explicit. But that means the politicians must be giving money for this" - Ismail Fajrie Alatas* (Merdeka News)

From above quotations, it appears that the mentioned religious groups are more into financial and political matter than religious, however, why they are using religious symbolisms? The answer is simple: they need followers and exploit them for their opportunist activities. Schwartz and Friederich on *Postmodern Thought and Criminological Discontent* (appears on *Theoretical Criminology* by George Bryan Vold, Thomas J. Bernard, Jeffrey B. Snipes; 2002) explains that the principal source of the domination in society is control of language system, because the words and phrases that people use to convey meaning are not neutral endeavors but support dominant views of the world, whether the people who use those languages know it or not (Milovanovic, 1993).

In the end, from postmodern view of criminology, these 'religious groups' are only opportunists masking themselves under religious identity. They exploit the religion of Islam as an instrument of their capital and political purpose. The words and their actions are not expressing their real intents, only articulated to match their organizations' identities. Thus, since we cannot accuse them of fraud because they are also submitting to the Islamic practices, it is safe to categorize them as *'Religious Opportunist Group'* instead.

**Discoursing Religion Industrial Complex**

Based on previous chapter, where socio-cultural background in Indonesia is accommodative for the opportunist, it is clear that in order to embrace the majority of Indonesian, you have to study their belief systems and how these beliefs shape and influence their behavior. What is the majority of people in Indonesia chose to believe in terms of religion? Islam dominated Indonesia's belief system so far, and as a result, studying the socio-cultural of moslem become a necessity. The importance of studying their socio-cultural background is so that the opportunists, be it religious groups or others far more influential in the social hierarchy, could adapt themselves according to how moslem usually interact, in which affecting the moslem perception and eventually acknowledged those opportunists as one of them. This approach is explained in symbolic interactionism theory, which is from *Sociology: Understanding a Diverse Society*, Margaret L. Andersen and Howard Francis Taylor (2007) analyzes society by addressing the subjective meanings that people impose on objects, events, and behaviors. According to symbolic interactionists, people behave based on what they believe, not just on what is objectively true. Thus, society is considered to be *socially constructed* through human interpretation. People interpret one another's behavior and these interpretations form social bonds. Let's underline the last sentence: *'People interpret one another's behavior and these interpretations form social bonds.'* It is without a doubt show how important interaction through symbolic meanings could change people perception and increase the probability of opportunists' exploit on that area.

Indonesia, luckily, provides an easy accommodation in the socio-cultural sphere, in relation with people's primary faith, which is Islam. What makes Indonesia an effortless target is that this third world developing country suffers a lot of problematical crisis which make a lot of people, especially from middle class and below, seeking for a shelter in the form of religious teachings. It is proven that religious practices affect the people who endure the structural injustice. Human Right Watch Asia on *China: State Control of Religion* explained that Religion's ritual interested these poor people who have nothing enjoyable in their life. Poor and sick people have nowhere to go (because of their financial limitation) except plead to God to cure their disease as in their religious belief, illness is somehow connected with the "devil". So in order to cast away their plague caused by the devil, they seek help from religion. In Indonesia, there are several famous councils holding the ritual of *pengajian* every week, usually attended by the members or public who are interested, and because of the charismatic leader and uncomplicated process of becoming member, their popularity rapidly grown.

***

## The Silent Victim

If we discourse this phenomenon from constitutive criminology, a flagship of the emerging postmodernism, notions of structural and cultural contexts are also count. As offered by Milovanovic:

> *"The essence of the constitutive argument is that crime and its control cannot be separated from the totality of the discursively ordered, structural and cultural contexts in which it is produced."*

Where does structural context play its part? Let's focus first on the specific relationship between Religious Opportunist Group and their follower. Every organization has its hierarchic structure; furthermore, the most common structure is obviously in a form of pyramid. The leader, in this case Habib, is the highest authority figure on Religious Opportunist Group; he decides the fate of his organization and apparently his figure is also significant as the organization image depends on Habib's charismatic persona. Therefore, all his words are automatically considered the utmost important and could implicitly means a form of command. By all means, his underlings and followers would act according to Habib wish, whether they like it or not, agree with it or not. Note that there is also exist the term of "symbolic violence" which according to Bordieu (*Constitutive Criminology: The Maturation of Critical Theory*, Stuart Henry and Dragan Milovanovic; 1991):

> *"gentle, invisible form of violence, which is never recognized as such, and is not so much undergone as chosen, the violence of credit, confidence, obligation, personal loyalty, hospitality, gifts, gratitude, piety…"*

Suppressed by silence, this pervasive domination is itself frozen in the past as *custom, pre-law,* and *law* of multiplex relations.

Needless to say, the lowest structure of those Religious Opportunist Groups' hierarchy are bound by these silent law and have no choice than to obey the leader's command. This is where they are vulnerable of being violated and exploited. In exception of financial matter, sometimes these opportunist groups also secretly force their members to engage in sexual activity (which is opposing their fundamental view of Islam where sexual intercourse is forbidden between same sex or unmarried couple). Below is the transcript of recent criminal news about Majelis Nurul Mustofa leader, Habib Hasan caught committing sexual harassment to his male disciples, reported by Tempo Interktif[16] news media portal:

> *"Police Investigators today re-examine Taklim Assembly (Majelis Taklim) leader Nurul Musthofa, Hasan Bin Jafar Assegaf. Hasan came to the police around 10:30 in a long white coat, black slacks, glasses, and wearing a dark green cap. The examination related to the alleged sexual abuse reported by a former student of Hasan."*

Habib Hasan's organization is supposed to be following the Islamic fundamental teachings, yet the recent incident shows otherwise. What can we deduct from this phenomenon? *First*, this Religious Opportunist Group is not religious at all. Religious mentioned here is devoting their life to the Islamic teachings and its law. Simply said, religion is only a tool, as discoursed on the previous chapter about Religious Opportunist Group. Another report coming from Gatra[17] is a little bit detailed and explicit:

> *"... We were told to massage (him)' Mamat said when he met Gatra last Thursday, after complaining to the*

---

[16] http://www.tempo.co/read/news/2012/03/16/064390628/Polisi-Kembali-Periksa-Pimpinan-Nurul-Mustofa

[17] http://www.gatra.com/hukum/31-hukum/8755-qkami-disuruh-mijitinq

*KPAI. After massaging the feet, Mamat was offered to be cleaned from all desires..."*

*"... Mamat was asked to treat Hasan like his lover. 'Vent all your passion to me if you want me to guard your desire,' Hasan said, quoted by Mamat. Hasan claimed that his actions performed on his capacity of Wali. 'This is what wali did, I do this to suppress your desire so it won't go wild,' said Hasan..."*

It looks more like a homosexual cult than religious council, if we perceive Mamat (the victim) explanation about how Habib Hasan treated him. The fact that the leader and also the founder of this council engages on sexual activity which are banned from Islamic law, we should question his motives in establishing the organization from the first place. Therefore, back to the victim, not just the sexually abused but in general manners (the deceived followers), according to Henry and Millovanovich (1996) are suffering a massive traumatic damage, as explained below:

*"Human 'subject-as-victim' is viewed as a special case of the "recovering subject," still with untapped human potentiality but with a damaged faith in humanity. Victims are more entrenched; more disabled, and suffer loss. Victims suffer the pain of being denied their own humanity, the power to make a difference. The victim of crime is thus rendered a non person, a non human, or less complete being"*

The above explanation might a little bit excessive; nevertheless, what happened to the victim in this kind of violence is fitting to that description. Let's assume that people join a Religious Opportunist Group, oblivious to its opportunist side, simply because they want to learn and embrace themselves in Islamic teachings. Now that their expectations were ruined, not only that they would lose their trust to this certain organization, they would also mistrust all religious organization; be it opportunist or not. Furthermore, their faith to the religion is also tarnished, along with their faith to all the pilgrims, scholars, and maybe humanity in general. However what can they do, when the organization is still up and running? They cannot make any difference and thus, making them even more tormented.

## Social Exchange

In every trade, there must be something to offer and people in need for that certain offer; therefore exists social exchange in society. There are several perspectives of social exchange based on the review from Kwang-Kuo Hwang (2011) on *Foundations of Chinese Psychology: Confucian Social Relations*:

- Anthropologists perspective: individual is an 'economic man' or 'rational man'
- Homans' theory: all social interactions are governed by, and hence can be analyzed in terms of, the same operant learning principles as those which explain the social behaviors of human beings: success proposition, stimulus proposition, value proposition, deprivation – satiation proposition, and aggression – approval proposition.
- Blau's theory: social exchange is fundamentally different from economic exchange in which the goods exchanged have clear market prices, the transaction regulated by explicit or implicit formal contractual rules that define the precise obligations incurred by both parties, and one may obtain his/her profit immediately following the transaction. Social exchanges will be judged by the subjective value of the goods or service, as well as the social approval obtained. Social exchange entails reliance upon such emergent properties as mutual trust allowing one to make substantial investment.

From mentioned theories of social exchange, the one researcher sees fit with Indonesia's social circumstances is from Blau's theory, which is clearly seen more *capital* oriented. In Indonesia case, especially, this very case of Religion Industrial Complex, there are people who will pay in exchange of a service done by the other. For example politicians, in order to reach their sphere in broader audience they will need a tool to execute that. This is where Religious Opportunist Groups play their part. This opportunist groups, however, need money to finance their organization and personal wealth, so they are willing to join along with the politicians trade offer. What is the service and what kind of payment? From previous chapter we already discourse that based on the published news articles and analyzing their movement, we can consider their service would be as a political agent in campaigning certain candidates. The targeted audience is supposed to be those groups' followers at least, and general public the most. Last is the payment, what kind of payment does the politicians offer? This is almost certainly money. Organization leader, often called Habib, are reported to have their wealth increased rapidly after their fame begin to rise, and so does their number of members. To maintain their organization, of course they need money, and their increased financial asset is the proof that they are also received 'donations' from external source other than from members or their various branch of business.

**Patron Client Relationship**

Social exchange which is happening between politicians and Religious Opportunist Groups also related to a patron client relationship. According to Merilee Serrill Grindle (1977) on *Bureaucrats, Politicians, and Peasants in Mexico: A Case Study in Public Policy*, patron client is an enduring dyadic bond based upon informally arranged personal exchanges of resources between actors of unequal status. The objective of each actor is to achieve certain goals by offering resources he controls or has access to in exchange for resources he does not control. Thus, the identifying characteristics of the patron client linkage are:

- An informal or nonlegally binding
- Personal or face-to-face relationship
- Involving an exchange of valued resources
- Between actors of unequal status
- Persists through time

From above points, we can try to compare it with how religious opportunists groups and politicians involved in the social exchange, and patron client relationship to be exact:

| Patron Client Characteristics | Relationship Between Religious Opportunist Group and Politicians |
|---|---|
| Informal and non-legal | Informal, as religious opportunists group are supposed to maintain their neutrality according to their 'religious' teachings' façade. Politicians are also vulnerable of being accused of logrolling if they are publicly formalizing this relationship. In terms of legality, religious opportunists groups are listed under *religious* organization, not *political* organization, thus this would remain illegal. In the case of police and Religious Opportunist Group, it is automatically considered illegal. |
| Personal or face-to-face relationship | Usually between the leader of the organization and politicians. Since this relationship is informal and non legal, they need to communicate face to face about their dealings. Especially if the relationship is between police and religious opportunists group; if they are caught doing illegal agreement then the accountability of the police would be tarnished. |

| | |
|---|---|
| Involving an exchange of valued resources | From the Religious Opportunist Group's side, the resource is obviously their mass followers, the bigger the better it would sell. From the politicians, they usually offer financial assets, money, or even law immunity (if this is the case between religious opportunists group and the police). |
| Between actors of unequal status | Status of politicians and police are always hierarchically higher than the religious opportunists, both from their financial assets, political power, and authorities. |
| Persists through time | When there is a demand, there will always be something to offer; this is the basics of why symbiotic relationship like this never dies. |

**Table 1** Comparison between patron client and relationship between Religious Opportunist Group and politician

Grindle (1977) explains that the relationship is entered into and sustained because each actor values things which the other provides and which the others cannot provide for themselves, as seen in how the relationship between Religious Opportunist Groups and politicians have something to offer for each other. However, the exchange is usually not immediate; the relationship is understood to be ongoing one in which the support of one binds the other in obligation until a future circumstances provides the opportunity to reciprocate. In addition, the exchange typically involves many aspects of the lives of the actors; it is a multifunctional relationship in which the actors call upon each other for a wide variety of favors affecting all aspects of their lives. The linkage between exchange partners is frequently 'institutionalized' through ritual coparenthood and godfathership. This situations explains the *'attack dog'* FPI and his master: police. For reminder, below are the articles published by several news media of FPI – Police relationship:

*"... Reported that FPI was used by the police to attack United States Embassy Jakarta on February 2006. The police utilized FPI as 'attack dog' so people would not blame police anymore on human rights infringement..." (Pedoman News)*

*"...FPI representative Muharman further claimed that if they are said to be Police's right hand men, then it is only for the sake of virtue towards society..." (Tempo Interaktif)*

In patron client relationship, the patron has great ability to obtain compliance from the client. No less important, however, is the ability of the subordinate to exert influence on the behavior of the superior because of his control over valued resources.

## Hegemonic Violence

In the theory of Hegemony, when Gramsci speaks of the state acting as domination, the state has incorporated certain corporatist interests and exercises its power to maintain these interests by keeping the subaltern social groups fragmented and passive within civil society. This represents a situation in which the definition and expansion of hegemony is enabled by the state's ability to fragment the operations of civil society and therefore its influence on political society (Richard Howson, *Hegemony: Studies in Consensus and Coercion*; 2008). From brief description above, how can we know that there is also exists hegemonic kind of violence? First is to analyze through its symbolic attributes.

***

## Symbolic Violence

Locating violence in hegemonic phenomenon is not always easy. Injustice and incapacitation in order to suppress the less dominant class are no longer executed through coercive means like on the feudal era. Moreover in Indonesia, after the people went from the strict new order to the reformation era and now democratic, repression is always detested by Indonesians. Considering this fact, hegemonic violence, if studied through usual method might not detailed enough; therefore, in this circumstance symbolic violence is used for the main analytical tool, along with discursive method.

Symbolic violence as explained by Stuart Henry and Dragan Millovanovic on *Constitutive Criminology: The Maturation of Critical Theory* (*Criminology* Volume 29 Number 2; 1991) is the:

> *"Gentle, invisible form of violence, which is never recognized as such, and is not so much undergone as chosen, the violence of credit, confidence, obligation, personal loyalty, hospitality, gifts, gratitude, piety…"*

The notion of gentle, invisible form of violence is the utmost important matter in finding the violence element in this hegemonic country. For example, how Religious Opportunist Groups, even though some of them already alleged by several misdemeanor, still invincible to the law. It is because they are hiding behind the religion mask, and choose to carry out their opportunist actions very carefully in order to deceive the masses. Not to mention their patron client relationship with politicians, even the police. Now for the bigger picture, please note that these Religious Opportunist Groups are also one of the pawns, carefully controlled by the Elite, in order to secure their hegemonic position in this country.

Who are the elites and who are their pawns? How many of them? These questions are always emerged regarding this hegemonic violence topic. This research, however, only focused on the possibility of its existence, using postmodern paradigm, in reading the faint trace of violence symbolism in relation with hegemony. Religious Opportunist Group is a perfect investment, in term of *power to dominate others*; this asset would benefit the hegemonic system by magnifying differences between each hierarchy. The elites or investors, control all class below them using their 'assets' which is one of them is Religious Opportunist Group. This practice is to prevent sub dominant class revolt and disturb the structure of class pyramid.

So who are violated in this practice? The answer is people. Be it all citizens in Indonesia or those religious opportunists' followers. They are oblivious to the scheme which is surrounding them and they cannot fight back. On the case where FPI asked their followers to support certain presidential candidate, it appeared as if there was no coercive action implemented. Nevertheless, in symbolic violence, there are also notions of '*violence of credit, confidence, obligation, personal loyalty, hospitality, gifts, gratitude, piety...*' (Henry, Millovanovich; 1991), in which even though the Habib did not explicitly command his followers, the followers are still obliged to do what he asked, as a part of their loyalty towards FPI. So does with the case of sexual harassment committed by Habib Hasan from Nurul Musthofa. All victims in the beginning were realized that the practice was wrong, but they chose to obey and let themselves abused instead.

In bigger scope, we are all victim. The fact that those religious opportunists are logrolling with politicians, how they are invincible to the law, how their leader financial are growing from members' and *donation* money, how they maintain a patron client relationship with the police, and how we are all suppressed and limited into advancing to the upper hierarchy; exploited and used for capital. Disinformation through forcing schematic consciousness planted by the elites is sacrificing the oblivious people; religious organizations with hidden agenda are built, masking their true intentions of benefitting the ruling class.

***

## Victim of Structural Violence

On *Violence, Peace, and Peace Research* journal, Galtung (1969) explains structural violence as a term firstly used on the 1960s era. That very term relates to a form of violence in a systemic technique where certain social structure or social institution harming people by preventing them to fulfill their needs. Through previous part, symbolic violence inside hegemonic system are found; and it is, one way or another, have a great relevancy with the above description of structural violence. People from sub dominant class are the victim, as quoted from

Merdeka.com[18] interview with Ismail F. Alatas which indicates the social class of some Religious Opportunist Groups' followers:

> *"We must remember that part of this assembly consists of people from suburb Jakarta, from Citayam, Depok, and from everywhere. They are all never have a place in this increasingly bourgeoisie capital town."*

> *"I for example, can go to nightclubs because I have money, have a car. However, they might unable to afford. 100 thousands rupiahs are still overpriced."*

However, because they are oblivious to the plot schemed by the opportunist groups, these followers often follows dreadful order from the leader and violate others. Another quotes from Ismail F. Alatas interview from merdeka.com:

> *"Because of the convoy, I failed to get into clubs and cafes. So this is like the embodiment of the people who are usually excluded, now dominating the area."*

> *"Sometimes there are intentional moves. (Habib) Hasan suddenly gather his council in New Year's Eve in Kemang. That was intentional."*

---

[18] http://www.merdeka.com/khas/ismail-f-alatas-2-majelis-wadah-eksistensi-warga-pinggiran.html

What they did can promote fascism and racism, without them even knowing. For example people from low class and sub dominant are being limited in term of access trough several recreational places in Jakarta because of this, resulting their position in society is getting worse.

However, their spiritual needs are also violated by the arrival of religious opportunists groups, who perform as if their motives are only spreading the Islamic teachings. Some of the behaviorally radicals are even become some kind of *soldier of fortune* by attacking public places, causing chaos and promote fascism towards the people. People are also politically deceived. Logrolling everywhere, corrupt politicians maintaining their patron client relationship with the opportunists; so they can still govern the people.

***

## Criminal Justice Industrial Complex

The conception of Religion Industrial Complex is coming from the idea of this idea by Richard Quinney's *Criminal Justice Industrial Complex*, which in the book titled *Criminology* he wrote about criminal justice industrial complex as a phenomenon where criminal justice is used for business opportunity with unnecessary purchases of criminal prevention tools and technology. Symbiotic relationship between government and industrial sector will always maintained in motion with the expanding monopoly sector. However, this book replaces the *criminal justice* with *religion*, as its main commodity of the industry.

The notion of Industry here is that there are people who treat religion in businesslike manner. Exploiting the dysfunction, which is a form of *sanctuary* for the oppressed people, religion then turned out to be a promising asset. Hence, the capital player needs a device to execute this work. And that is when Religious Opportunist Group come to play; their symbiotic relationship and patron client affiliation with the police, and not to mention their huge number of followers, is very ideal for this dirty job. However, the products sold are varies; for capital, political, merchandise and as previously stated, this is also a very good device for maintaining hegemony.

***

In the end, what is the term 'Religion Industrial Complex' actually mean? It is related to the use of religion as a commodity, and sold in a variety of forms, such as:

- Capital
- Political
- Hegemony

Nonetheless, a device or media is needed in order to shape those forms. And this book is using the example of how Religious Opportunist Group could become one of the perfect tools for that purpose.

Discoursing this 'Religion Industrial Complex' phenomenon is not a simple task; it needs a correct method in order to construct and analyze the whole aspect, especially since the form of violence here are very soft and mostly invisible. Discursive method is proven effective; however, the symbolic traits of the crime and interactions have to be analyzed slowly in order to deduct the true meanings of what it is hiding behind a certain event.

From how this research turns out, this book conclude several points based upon the research purpose:

- Indonesia's socio-cultural background is very accommodative for this injustice practice of Religion Industrial Complex
- Religious Opportunists Groups exists as one of the tools used for executing Religion Industrial Complex scheme
- Religious Opportunists Groups exploit religion in order to optimize its follower counts and gain financial profit
- Religious Opportunists Groups engage in social exchange and patron client relationship with politicians and police
- Violence which apparent in Religion Industrial Complex is symbolic
- Religion commoditization exists in various forms such as capital, political, and hegemony
- Hegemonic violence is causing a lot of unaware victims; especially sub-dominant class

The last part is the conception about Religion Industrial Complex. It is related to the use of religion as a commodity, and sold in a variety of forms: capital, political, and hegemony.

Nonetheless, a device or media is needed in order to shape those forms. And this book is using the example of how Religious Opportunist Group could become one of the perfect tools for that purpose.

Based on the points concluded on the previous segment, this book would suggest a few recommendations to the general public, especially since most of them are situated in the very bottom of hierarchical class pyramid:

1. People must realize of the existence of Religious Opportunist Groups and avoid themselves getting victimized.
2. Studying symbolic violence, symbolic interactionism, and patron client might help in assessing the malevolent traits of Religious Opportunist Group, so precautions could be considered; since those opportunists groups' actions are mostly through symbolic means.
3. Alertness of this whole hegemonic situations are also needed since the repression is very faint and probably undetected, thus, be careful of the potential provocation planted to disrupt the people through hate, racism, fascism, and many more.
4. If it is too late and already victimized by this cruel hegemonic Religion Industrial Complex system, never hesitate to voice out and quit, never fall for the concept of obedience, loyalty, and such; since they are all constructed by design.
5. Awareness is the most important key; aware of the surroundings, always question and criticize dubious occurrences, because there are a lot more dangerous hegemonic tools outside, waiting to be unfold.

## About The Author

Hesti Wulandari was born in December 18th 1989. She holds a Bachelor's Degree of Criminology from Universitas Indonesia at the year of 2012. This book is based on her undergraduate research book.

Hesti enjoys nature and is very fond of ancient philosophy. She plans to continue her study towards Master Degree and contribute more to her country, Indonesia.

Hesti can be reached through e-mail: hesti@windowslive.com

## Books

Bocock, Robert. *Hegemony*. Routledge, 1986

Della Porta, Donatella and Vanucci, Alberto. *Corrupt Exchanges: Actors, Resources, and Mechanism of Political Corruption: Social Problems and Social Issues*. Aldine Transaction, 1999

Giligan, James. *Violence: Reflections on a National Epidemic*. Vintage, 1997

Gramsci, Antonio. *Selections from the Prison Notebooks*. International Publishers Co, 1971

Haugaard, Mark and Lentner, Howard H. *Hegemony and Power: Consensus and Coercion in Contemporary Politic*. Lexington Books, 2006

Marx, Karl and Engel, Friedrich. *Manifesto of the Communist Party*. Wilder Publications, 2007

Marx, Karl and Engel, Friedrich. *On Religion*. Foreign Languages Pub. House, 1957

Marx, Karl and Engel, Friedrich. *The German Ideology*. International Publishers Co, 1970

Marx, Karl and Raines, John. *Marx on Religion*. Temple University Press, 2002

Marx, Karl. *A Contribution to the Critique of Hegel's Philosophy of Right*. Deutsch-Französische Jahrbücher, 1844

Quinney, Richard. *Criminology: Analysis and Critique of Crime in America*. Little Brown, 1975

Tischler, Henry L. *Introduction to Sociology*. Wadsworth Publishing, 2006

## Journals

Akhter, Muhammad Yeahia and Huque, Ahmed Shafiqul. *The Ubiquity of Islam: Religion and Society in Bangladesh*. Pacific Affairs, University of British Columbia, 1987

Bilings, Dwight B. *Religion as Opposition: A Gramscian Analysis*. The University of Chicago Press, 1990

Center for Religious and Cross-cultural Studies (CRCS). *Laporan Tahunan Kehidupan Beragama Di Indonesia Tahun 2008*. Universitas Gadjah Mada, 2008

Firth, Raymond. *Spiritual Aroma: Religion and Politics*. Blackwell Publishing, 1981

Fox, Jonathan. *Religion and State Failure: An Examination of the Extent and Magnitude of Religious Conflict from 1950 to 1996*. Sage Publications, Ltd. 2004

Iannaccone, Laurence R. *Introduction to the Economics of Religion*. American Economic Association, 1998

Liddle, William. *The Islamic Turn in Indonesia: A Political Explanation*. Association for Asian Studies, 1996

Lindsay, D. Michael. *Evangelical in the Power Elite: Elite Cohesion Advancing a Movement*. American Sociological Association, 2008

Schoenfeld, Eugen. *Militant and Submissive Religions: Class, Religion and Ideology*. The British Journal of Sociology, 1992

Scott, Shaunna L and Billings, Dwight B. *Religion and Political Legitimation*. Annual Reviews, 1994

Veer, Peter Van Der. *Religion in South Asia*. Annual Reviews, 2002

Wood, Richard L. *Religious Culture and Political Action*. American Sociological Association, 1999